THE HOLISTIC CAT
A Complete Guide to Natural Health Care

Holly Mash

THE CROWOOD PRESS

First published in 2014 by
The Crowood Press Ltd
Ramsbury, Marlborough
Wiltshire SN8 2HR

www.crowood.com

British Library Cataloguing-in-Publication Data
A catalogue record for this book is available from the British Library.

ISBN 978 1 84797 780 9

Disclaimer
The author and publisher do not accept any responsibility in any manner whatsoever for any error or omission, or any loss, damage, injury, adverse outcome, or liability of any kind incurred as a result of the use of any of the information contained in this book, or reliance upon it. If in doubt about any aspect of holistic treatment, readers are advised to seek professional advice. For simplicity, throughout this book cats are referred to as 'she'.

This book is dedicated to my darling husband and our family.

Typeset by Jean Cussons Typesetting, Diss, Norfolk
Printed and bound in India by Replika Press Pvt Ltd

CONTENTS

'On a Cat, Ageing'
by Sir Alexander Gray

He blinks upon the hearth-rug,
And yawns in deep content,
Accepting all the comforts
That Providence has sent.

Louder he purrs and louder,
In one glad hymn of praise
For all the night's adventures,
For quiet restful days.

Life will go on for ever,
With all that cat can wish;
Warmth and the glad procession
Of fish and milk and fish.

Only – the thought disturbs him –
He's noticed once or twice,
The times are somehow breeding
A nimbler race of mice.

1 INTRODUCING COMPLEMENTARY THERAPIES

'When the minds of the people are closed and wisdom is locked out, they remain tied to disease.'

The Yellow Emperor's Classic of Medicine (220 BC)

HOLISTIC MEDICINE

In holistic veterinary medicine we consider the whole of each patient, not just the symptom or condition they have presented with. This means that an in-depth consultation, usually taking an hour or more, is an important part of most forms of holistic medicine. Your cat's family background, past and present medical history, as well as diet and daily routine, will all be explored and discussed. The holistic vet will also ask you about your cat's personality and any individualizing characteristics of the presenting complaint. The details of any diagnostic tests that have been performed may also be of assistance. Finally, as well as observing the cat carefully throughout the consultation, they will also perform a full physical examination of your cat.

'The whole is more than the sum of its parts,' said the Greek philosopher Aristotle, neatly describing the general principle of holism.

Mind and body

The strong link between physical and emotional health is understood in holistic medicine. The interrelationship between mind and body has been accepted for centuries in traditional forms of medicine all over the world. In modern veterinary practice it is most easily compared to a branch of medicine called psychoneuroendocrinoimmunology (PNEI). This investigates the links between an animal's mind (psycho), its nervous and hormonal systems (neuro-endocrine), and its immune system. A holistic approach to healing recognizes that the emotional, mental, spiritual and physical elements of each individual comprise a totality, and the aim is to treat the whole patient in this context. It concentrates on the cause of the illness as well as the symptoms.

INTEGRATED HEALTH CARE

Conventional veterinary treatment is, of course, a vital part of our toolbox of treatment options for your cat. How else, apart from with surgery, are we going to fix her broken tail or neuter her? In-deed, antibiotics are often crucial in helping us combat otherwise life-threatening infections. The aim of 'integrated veterinary medicine' is to use each form of treatment, whether it is herbal, homeopathic, acupuncture,

Holistic medicine considers the mind and body as a whole.

antibiotics or surgery, where it is most appropriate. Therefore, by widening the scope of possible treatment options for your cat, she will have a greater range of healing possibilities in any given circumstance. With an increasing number of disease-causing organisms becoming resistant to modern drugs, and a growing number of chronic conditions affecting today's cats, it is little wonder that there is a shift towards holistic and natural treatment. This is indeed the future for health care for your cat in the twenty-first century. The key to integrated medicine is to use complementary and conventional medicine in conjunction, wherever possible. For example, a homeopathic remedy may be used to speed up healing after orthopaedic surgery has been performed to fix a fractured tail, or Bach Flower remedies used alongside behavioural modification techniques. However, don't forget that each of the complementary therapies outlined here is also a complete healing system in its own right and in many cases will be best suited as a sole form of holistic treatment for your cat.

This chapter will review the most widely available and commonly used complementary treatments, explaining how they work and when they will be most useful. This will help you to know which particular complementary treatment will be best suited to your cat in a given situation.

HOMEOPATHY

Homeopathy is a system of medicine that stimulates the body's own self-healing mechanisms. It is based on the principle that 'like cures like', which has been called the 'law of similars'. This theory dates back to the days of Hippocrates and the Ancient Greeks in the fifth century BCE ('the majority of maladies can be cured by the same things that caused them'). However, it was only when the German physician Dr Samuel Hahnemann formulated it as a complete system of medicine in its own right in the early nineteenth century that homeopathy as we know it today was born.

How does it work?
Homeopathy acknowledges that the

body has a natural self-healing mechanism, called the 'vital force'. This can be considered as the energy in every living thing, that regulates the body and maintains health. Homeopathic remedies act to stimulate the vital force, and restore health in a gentle and natural manner. The most important principles in homeopathic medicine are as follows:

The law of similars
Diseases are treated with remedies that in a healthy individual would produce symptoms similar to those that they are used to treat. For example, Allium cepa, the homeopathic remedy made from red onion, is commonly used to treat symptoms of streaming eyes and nose: the same signs that you get when you slice a red onion. One way of understanding how homeopathic remedies stimulate self-healing is to compare them to how a tuning fork works. Thus, when the correct remedy is given to a patient it will resonate with her body and help it to re-tune to her normal, healthy frequency. The principle of 'like cures like' is at the heart of homeopathic treatment because only the most precisely matched homeopathic remedies will resonate with the body and stimulate healing in this way. This is the

reason behind the lengthy and detailed case taking. To make the best 'match' between symptoms and remedy, in other words the most effective prescription, the homoeopath needs to know all about your cat and her unique set of symptoms. Armed with this information, they will consult their materia medica – books that describe the healing powers of each remedy – and through this process of analysis, known as 'repertorization', they will be able to find the remedy that most exactly matches your cat's symptoms.

The minimum effective dose
Homeopathic remedies are mainly derived from plants, for example arnica and calendula, but others come from minerals, and others still from animal sources. A process called 'potentization' manufactures them. This consists of serially diluting the active component in a solution, and vigorously agitating it at each stage. This process results in a remedy that is at once energetically active, or 'potent', but also highly diluted. The 'potency' is a measure of the 'strength' of a homeopathic remedy. It is denoted by a 'c' or 'x' after a number, for example 30c or 6x. These letters relate to the two most common potency scales used in homeopathy:

Homeopathic remedies need to be stored carefully.

the centesimal scale (c), where there has been a dilution of one in a hundred at each stage in the manufacture, or the decimal scale (x), where the dilution is one in ten. However paradoxical it sounds, the more dilute the remedy the more potent it becomes. For example, a 30c remedy is stronger than a 12c remedy. This is because, although it is more diluted, the remedy has also gone through more of the activating 'succussions' in its manufacture. The remedies range from low potency 6c to high potency 200c and 1M (a different scale altogether, used for very high potency remedies). Most everyday uses of homeopathy for cats use 12c or 30c potency remedies.

Aconitum napellus *(monkshood),* the homeopathic remedy for shock.

Treating the individual, not the disease
The homoeopath will always need to build up a complete picture of each individual patient through taking a detailed case history, and by careful observation in the consultation. They will ask about the history of the illness or condition, and when it started, as well as about your cat's other medical history apart from her current complaint. They will ask for details about her family background, and where you obtained her, her everyday routines, her character and personality, as well as any factors that make your cat's presenting complaint either better or worse. No detail is too insignificant for the veterinary homoeopath, as the most unusual symptom or characteristic of your cat may be the key that helps them to find the most suitable remedy for her.

Obstacles to cure
This is another guiding principle in homeopathy and means that any factor in the patient's life that may be hampering the action of the homeopathic remedies should be removed whenever possible. This relates to the holistic idea that unless contributory factors that affect your cat's overall health, such as nutrition, vaccination, environmental and emotional factors, are addressed, then the homeopathic treatment cannot work to its full potential.

What is it used for?
Homeopathy is a system of medicine in its own right, suitable for treating a wide range of conditions, from the sudden to the long standing. Home treatment is valuable for a range of mild ailments and as a first aid measure, such as using arnica for bruises, calendula cream for cuts and grazes, and ruta for strains and sprains (*see* Chapter 9). However, in-depth consultation and referral to a veterinary homoeopath is also suitable for ongoing or chronic conditions, such as allergies, urinary tract disease or cancer. Finally, homeopathy should be considered as a treatment option in conditions where conventional medicine may not be possible, or indeed where there is no other treatment available.

STORAGE OF HOMEOPATHIC REMEDIES

Careful storage of remedies is important. Keep them away from any highly aromatic substances (such as mint, lavender or garlic), magnetic fields, electromagnetic radiation (such as mobile phones and computers), as well as extreme temperatures and direct sunlight. Equally, try not to handle homeopathic remedies.

How to administer homeopathic remedies

Homeopathic medicines are called 'remedies' and each remedy can be bought in whichever formulation is easiest for you to give to your cat: tablets, liquids or powders. Often liquids are easiest to administer to cats; simply place a dose (one to two drops) on the tip of her nose and she will then lick it off. Homeopathic remedies are best given to your cat between meals, in other words not with her food, nor within about twenty minutes of any other medicines. Tip tablets directly from the lid of the container into your cat's mouth (but if you are placing a drop on her nose then using your finger is fine). These special recommendations are given because the subtle healing properties of the remedies can be easily over-powered and negated. However, if you are having real problems getting your cat to take a homeopathic remedy, then it can be given with a little plain food and it is highly likely to work just as well.

Dosage

Most commonly indicated remedies that you may have reason to use for your cat will be 12c or 30c potency. One pill or tablet is one dose, and in liquid formulations one dose is one to two drops. How often you give the remedy, and the potency that you use, rather than the number of tablets or drops given at any one time, is the key to homeopathic dosing. Homeopathic remedies are always given one dose at a time, waiting for the response in the patient after each one. A general rule of thumb is to match how often you give the remedy to how quickly the problem started, dosing more frequently for sudden onset complaints and less often for long-standing ones. The other important thing is to stop dosing when you see a change in the patient's symptoms – whether this is a mental and emotional improvement or a physical one. This is an indication that your cat's self-healing mechanisms have been stimulated into action and the remedy has done its job. You may well see an improvement in your cat's mental and emotional state before you see an improvement in her physical symptoms.

Integrated treatment

There are no side effects to homeopathic treatment. However, you should be aware of the possibility of what is called an aggravation. This is when your cat's symptoms become temporarily worse immediately following the first one or two doses of a homeopathic remedy. It is not common and usually means that she was given too high a potency or that she is especially sensitive to the remedy. If your cat suffers from an aggravation do not give her any further doses. The symptoms will usually settle within twenty-four to forty-eight hours, and then she will start to get better.

If your cat is having any conventional medications concurrently with homeopathic treatment, it is important to follow the advice of your veterinary homoeopath. She should be receiving integrated care, which means that your cat is given the best and most appropriate form of treatment for any given condition.

How to find a qualified practitioner
Fully qualified homeopathic vets have the letters VetMFHom after their name. The governing body for veterinary homoeopaths is the Faculty of Homeopathy (*see* Useful Addresses at the back of this book).

HERBAL MEDICINE
Herbalism is the most widely used and ancient form of medical practice still in use today. It has been integral to the medical traditions of cultures in China and India as well as Western Europe for thousands of years. One of the earliest records of animals being treated with herbs was in the Ayurvedic Nakul Samhita, a treatise written between 4500 and 1600 BCE, concerning mainly horses and elephants. Since then, veterinary botanical medicine has grown and spread, and as recently as the 1960s herbal formulas were listed in veterinary textbooks and considered

The herbal remedy Echinacea purpurea.

CATS AND SALICYLATES

It is important to know that aspirin (acetylsalicylic acid) and other salicylate-containing drugs and herbs (such as white willow bark, meadowsweet and feverfew) are highly toxic to cats. This is because cats have different metabolic pathways in their livers and so detoxify salicylate much more slowly than humans and dogs do. Differences in a cat's metabolism relate to its super-carnivore status and having a diet that is geared towards existing on almost 100 per cent meat, with a very limited capacity to metabolize plants (i.e. herbs). This hypersensitivity to herbs is why it's very important only ever to give your cat medication that is prescribed by your vet and clearly labelled for her.

---

as orthodox medicine. Currently there is a worldwide drive to source plants with medicinal properties and to learn traditional herbal treatments from indigenous peoples. In fact many global pharmaceutical companies are actively searching for new wonder drugs in the world's dwindling rainforests and jungles. Special care, however, must be taken when using any herbal medicines in cats because they have some unique metabolic pathways that make them particularly susceptible to toxicity from certain plant compounds.

How does it work?
The majority of our modern drugs, including veterinary ones, are derived from plants, and Nature's healing properties are well known. Herbs provide us with a

great variety of pharmacologically active ingredients, called phytochemicals. They are also categorized in western herbal medicine according to their action on the body, some acting on a particular organ, others as whole body tonics. In addition, herbs can act to help the body to detoxify itself through the promotion of urination (diuretics) and bowel movements (purgatives), or to support the immune system (adaptogens). Different cultures have different ways of categorizing herbal medicines, but the uses remain the same.

Nature's medicine chest provides the basis for most medicines we use today. For example, the active principle in the painkiller morphine derives from the poppy, that of the heart drug digitalis from the foxglove; more recently an important cancer drug has been derived from the periwinkle. However, these pharmaceutical medicines contain only a single active component, or extract, of the plant, whereas in herbal medicine the whole plant is used. This is because the rest of the herb provides important nutrients and phytochemicals that support the rest of the body. Thus, using the whole leaf, root, flower and seed ensures that the variety of compounds that occur naturally in the plant are available for the body to use, giving it a holistic action without the side effects that refined pharmaceutical compounds can cause. One such example is the dandelion, because a dandelion leaf is rich in minerals, including potassium. When it is used as a diuretic it naturally replenishes the body with this mineral, whereas the diuretic drug, with its narrow scope of action, does not.

What is it used for?
Herbs can be used effectively as medicines in their own right, or in conjunction with conventional drugs. Used in a holistic manner, herbs act to gently stimulate the body's self-healing mechanisms. Alternatively, herbs can be used in a superficial manner, to get rid of symptoms without addressing the underlying cause. Finally, it shouldn't be forgotten that herbs are also foods, with their culinary qualities being just as important as their medicinal ones. Some cats retain the natural instinct to self-medicate when they are feeling unwell and will seek out couch grass to chew, which seems to help them regurgitate a food that didn't agree with them or to bring up a hair-ball.

Administration and dosage of herbal medicines
Cats can be extra-sensitive to herbs owing to differences in their metabolic pathways that don't allow them to detoxify certain plants in the same way that dogs and other animals do. This is related to their being true carnivores and their bodies being poorly adapted to using plant material. In addition, be aware that individual cats can have allergies to certain plant families, and hence certain herbs (such as chamomile) may not be suitable for them.

Herbs can be given to your cat in a variety of different ways, but it's not easy as cats are such fussy creatures and can sniff out something unusual in their food at a hundred paces! Added to this challenge is the fact that they are uniquely susceptible to toxicity from certain herbs, which means that you have to be very careful, as well as cunning, when it comes to using herbal medicines for your cat. Part of the reason why cats are tricky to medicate is that they are very sensitive to the smell and taste of alcohol, and most herbal tinctures are alcohol based.

Cats love catnip (Nepeta cataria).

Glycerin-based tinctures are a more palatable option, and hence the preferred way of using herbal medicine for your cat. Another, less problematic, method may be to use herbal tablets or capsules containing either powdered dried herbs or freeze-dried extracts. Products formulated especially for cats should have the dosage on the label; otherwise your veterinary herbalist will guide you. Always begin with small doses, and see how your cat tolerates them, before increasing to

---

CATNIP

Cats inhabit a world where the sense of smell is crucial. A cat's nose is lined with millions of specialized odour-detecting cells. This is another of the reasons why catnip *(Nepeta cataria)* has such an effect on them, as they are so finely tuned to the language of scent. Scientists have studied cats' unique behavioural reactions to catnip and have linked them to a special chemical stimulus that it triggers in the their olfactory system, making them respond to its particular smell. These behaviours include chewing and sniffing as associated with feeding, rolling and rubbing as associated with female sexual behaviour and a type of kicking and pouncing associated with predation and play. Every cat responds to catnip slightly differently, with one or more types of behaviour being dominant, and occurring at every exposure to catnip or just occasionally. However, catnip has no effect at all on around 10 per cent of the cat population, thought to be due to a genetic variation. Although some progress has been made in identifying the reason why catnip is such a powerful herb for cats, the full story of how cats are affected by this amazing mint that is named after them is still largely unknown.

ESSENTIAL OILS AND AROMATHERAPY

Essential oils are the natural fragrant essences extracted from flowers (such as lavender), leaves (such as eucalyptus), bark, roots and berries. These concentrated scents have qualities which, when extracted or distilled, can benefit physical ailments and promote emotional well-being when used in aromatherapy or as a natural flea repellant, for example. However, due to the potential for toxicity if taken internally (a cat's liver cannot process the terpenes in alcohol), you should never use them for cats without professional guidance.

the required dose of any herbal medicine. Do not assume that human products can simply be given to your cat at a reduced rate; this is not the case and many herbal preparations are potentially toxic for cats. If you are using topical herbal creams and ointments, or one of the number of commercially available products, do check the ingredients carefully before you use them on your cat. This is because she is likely to lick some of it off, and you need to be sure it is safe if she does so.

The bottom line is that you should always consult a specialist herbalist vet before starting your cat on any herbal supplement or medicine. That way you won't get the wrong herb or the wrong dose, and you'll know it won't interfere with any other medicines she may be taking. This is very important.

Cats are very sensitive to essential oils.

Integrated treatment

Seeking the advice of a specialist vet is always essential when using any herbal medicine for your cat. This is because any herb has the potential to be harmful, as well as healing, especially in cats where their metabolism makes them uniquely susceptible to toxicity. Herbs can cause side effects, such as vomiting or diarrhoea, or your cat may have an allergic reaction to them. Herbs can also interact with any conventional medications and other supplements your cat may be taking. All of these are reasons for seeking veterinary guidance when using any herbs for your cat.

How to find a qualified practitioner

The British Association of Veterinary Herbalists represents veterinary surgeons trained in herbal medicine (*see* Useful Addresses at the back of this book).

HERBALISM AND HOMEOPATHY

These two forms of holistic medicine are often confused. This usually stems from the fact that many homeopathic remedies are derived from plants that are also used in herbal medicine. However, they are very different healing systems. Homeopathy is an energy-based system, whilst herbal medicine uses measurable amounts of the herb in its remedies. If you go wrong with homeopathy the worst that can usually happen is that your cat does not improve. But if you use the wrong herbs or the wrong dose in herbal medicine, then this could potentially be fatal. Thus it is essential to understand that these are two completely different branches of holistic medicine.

ACUPUNCTURE

Acupuncture originated several thousand years ago in East Asia, as a form of traditional Chinese medicine (TCM). Ancient records and clay models of horses with acupuncture points marked on them have been traced to this period. Western civilizations gradually adopted acupuncture practice until it gained major popularity as a complementary veterinary practice in the 1970s, with the establishment of the International Veterinary Acupuncture Society (IVAS).

How does it work?

Acupuncture is defined as the insertion of fine needles into specific points on the body. Not every cat will put up with having acupuncture, and it is really only suitable for cats with tolerant dispositions that enjoy being handled and made a fuss of. The principle of how acupuncture works can be explained by two very different theories, the western and the traditional Chinese. According to the western understanding of acupuncture the insertion of the needles triggers the release of a complex cascade of chemicals in the body, and causes a modification of the pain pathways in the brain and spinal cord. Both of these effects result in pain relief for the patient. In addition there are more generalized effects of acupuncture needling on the body. It has a regulatory effect on the cat's nervous and hormonal systems, as well as her circulatory, digestive and immune functions. Over the past thirty years there has been much research into acupuncture, leading to several well-accepted neurophysiological models for its mode of action. On a microscopic level it has been shown that acupuncture points can be differentiated from the surrounding skin. They have an increased number of nerve endings, blood vessels and immune system tissue, as well as a lowered electrical resistance.

East meets West

In TCM, acupuncture is just one element in a range of therapies used to restore health, including herbal medicine, breathing and movement exercises (Qiguong and Tai Qi), and attention to diet. Fundamental to the TCM understanding of health and disease is the concept of a vital energy called qi (pronounced 'chee'), which flows through the body along channels called meridians. Qi is maintained by yin and yang, the equal and opposite forces whose perfect balance keeps the body in harmony and health. Pain and disease are seen as a blockage of qi. Acupuncture points are the places along the meridians where the body's qi energy can be tapped into by the insertion of needles. This alters and re-balances the flow of qi, and hence restores health. Traditional Chinese medicine is based on the Taoist principles of seeing the body as a reflection of the universe. Philosophers understood the interrelationship between the universe and the human body as a continuous cycle of qi. They placed great importance on living a life in harmony with one's environment, balancing the active and the passive, the yin and yang. In the third and fourth centuries BCE doctors had to rely on their sense of sight, smell, taste, hearing and touch to diagnose and treat illness. Hence they formulated associations between the seasons, the weather and the physical lie of the land around them (the hills, mountains and rivers) with the inner workings of the body. This is the basis for the five-element theory, a common method of diagnosis and treatment in TCM.

Each acupuncture treatment is tailored to the individual patient, incorporat-

Acupuncture is used for pain relief.

ing the use of different points in order to harmonize their specific qi imbalance. Chinese herbs will often be used as part of your cat's TCM treatment alongside her acupuncture.

What is it used for?

Acupuncture is used to provide a natural form of pain relief for many conditions, most commonly those of the musculoskeletal system such as those associated with lameness and arthritis. It is also especially helpful for cats that either cannot be given conventional painkillers, or who suffer from side effects and hence cannot take them. However, traditional Chinese medicine and acupuncture are also

VARIATIONS ON ACUPUNCTURE

There are variations on the everyday 'dry needling' technique used in acupuncture that may be more useful in certain situations. Laser acupuncture employs infrared lasers to stimulate acupuncture points, and is a particularly useful technique for cats that do not tolerate needles. Electroacupuncture uses a pulse of electric current to stimulate the needles, and is most commonly used to treat paralysis.

a complete medical system in their own right and can therefore be indicated for the treatment of a wide range of medical problems. These commonly include skin conditions and immune system diseases.

Integrated treatment

Acupuncture is becoming increasingly accepted and integrated into conventional veterinary practice. This is due in large part to the fact that it can be understood within the framework of Western medicine. In other words you don't have to believe in the concept of qi to be able to explain how it works. Your regular vet as part of a routine appointment may give your cat acupuncture or may refer her to a specialist vet. Acupuncture should not be done if your cat is pregnant.

The acupuncture treatment itself consists of around eight to twelve ultra fine, sterile, single-use needles being inserted in various places on your cat's body. The acupuncturist would usually treat cats with them either sitting on a table or on their owner's lap, so that they feel more relaxed and comfortable. The needles are commonly left in place for between ten and fifteen minutes. In addition to relieving pain, acupuncture also has a sedative action on the body. Therefore some cats become quite relaxed and tranquil during the session as the needles stimulate the release of natural sedatives into their circulation. They may be a little sleepy or tired for up to twenty-four hours after a treatment, but this is not usually the case.

Whilst some cats are highly responsive to acupuncture and will show a marked improvement after just a single treatment, the majority of patients need several sessions before a change is seen. Acupuncture is usually done weekly for the first four sessions, reducing to less frequently after that, depending on the nature of the condition and the response of the patient. Many elderly, arthritic cats are treated every four to six weeks to help them remain comfortable. A minority of cats can be unresponsive to acupuncture and will not respond to treatment.

How to find a qualified practitioner

Vets trained in acupuncture will usually have gained their qualifications through either the International Veterinary Acupuncture Society (IVAS), in which case they will have a more traditional Chinese medicine approach to treatment, or they will have done a course through the Association of British Veterinary Acupuncturists (ABVA) (see Useful Addresses at the back of this book).

THE BACH FLOWER ESSENCES

The Bach flower remedies are a series of thirty-eight flower essences that are used to treat a wide range of emotional or behavioural problems in cats, as well as other animals. The best known is Rescue Remedy, used for shock.

Help your cat to relax using Bach flower remedies.

How do they work?

The Bach flower remedies were developed in the 1930s by Dr Edward Bach (pronounced Batch), a pioneering Harley Street surgeon and homoeopath, who wanted to find a gentle and natural way of healing. He sought a simple, safe way to restore harmony in the body through emotional well-being. After many years working with the flowers and trees in the Oxfordshire countryside where he lived, Dr Bach developed his series of flower remedies. They work on the same energetic or vibrational principles as homeopathic remedies and have an effect on the emotional and spiritual levels of the body, to stimulate self-healing. Bach flower remedies balance negative emotions, such as grief, anger and frustration, into positive ones, such as happiness and contentment. Each of the thirty-eight remedies helps to deal with a particular negative state of mind. Dr Bach understood the link between stress, emotions and illness when he said that there was no true healing unless there was a change in outlook, peace of mind and inner happiness. These flower essences do not use the physical material of the plant, like

The Bach Centre, home of Dr Edward Bach.

herbal medicines, but rather the essential energy that is found within the flower. It is this that represents their healing quality. Dr Bach's dream was for his system of thirty-eight flower remedies to be easy enough to prescribe and use so that people could use them for everyday situations at home. He wanted to give people the power to heal themselves, their own family and friends and those around them. Even though they were developed for use in people, Bach flower remedies have been used to treat animals for over fifty years.

Since Dr Bach's day, several different systems of flower essences have been developed, and are now used all over the world, from California to Australia. However, it seems most appropriate to use the Bach flower essences on British cats, as their bodies will be more attuned to the essence of our native wild flowers.

How are they made?
Dr Bach chose only those flowers that grew wild and uncultivated and were non-poisonous; he felt that the strength and purity of the plants was important. Their healing energy is extracted by simple methods that are still followed when the essences are made at the Bach Flower Centre today. A glass bowl is filled with pure water, and then the flowers are picked and floated on the water to cover the surface. This must be done on a clear sunny day when the flowers are in perfect bloom. The bowl is then left in the sunlight for three to four hours and the healing energy within the flowers is transferred into the water. This is then used as the basis of the flower essence, which is preserved in alcohol and bottled into the range that you can buy in most large pharmacies or health food shops. Due to the (albeit tiny amount of) alcohol

present, an even better solution for cats will be the range of Bach flower essences preserved in non-alcoholic media such as glycerin. Similarly there is an alcohol-free Rescue Remedy.

Put yourself in your cat's shoes
When you are using these flower essences for your cat you have to try to work out exactly which emotion or emotions she is feeling. This can obviously be a difficult business, as it is all too easy to anthropomorphize and misinterpret her signals. Therefore when we are using these thirty-eight flower remedies for cats, we need to remember to try to look at the situation from her point of view, and not just prescribe for the natural human emotion in a given situation. For example, bear in mind that what we think of as fearful or terrifying situations can be quite different from those of our cats. Imagine how terrified and panic-stricken cats can be about having their nails clipped. Here a remedy for extreme fear and terror may be applicable. It's also important to realize that there are some negative emotions that Dr Bach identified, such as bitterness and hatred, that would very rarely be attributed to a cat. Therefore animal treatment with flower essences can be complex and will involve a good insight into your cat's behaviour. If you can't work out what your cat is feeling, or if your combination of flower remedies has not worked in a given situation, you should consult a qualified Bach flower animal practitioner.

What are they used for?
The Bach flower remedies are used to treat emotional disturbances in cats. These can be, for example, trauma-related, or anxiety- and fear-based problems. They are often especially helpful for rescue cats that may have a traumatic past

Bach flower remedies are used to balance the emotions and can help anxious cats.

history. Examples of where Bach flower remedies are indicated include helping cats adjust to new situations, such as the arrival of a new baby into the family, or the introduction of a new pet. They are also used to help ease the transition between life stages, such as at weaning, sexual maturity and also in ageing. These flower remedies are a useful aid for calming anxieties such as those caused by multi-cat households or by neighbourhood cats. Bach flower remedies can also be used in treating grief states and for anxiety about travel or going to a cattery. Rescue Remedy is the best known of the Bach flower remedies and is a composite of five flower essences. It can be used to treat the shock and panic that normally arise in an emergency situation.

How to administer Bach flower remedies
Bach flower essences are liquid remedies, they are used diluted and given by mouth, usually on food. If you have seen a Bach flower practitioner they will have made

---

POPULAR USES OF BACH FLOWER REMEDIES

Star of Bethlehem – used for the after-effects of shock; useful for rescue cats.

Aspen – used to treat fear of the unknown, for nervy, jumpy cats.

Walnut – used to help your cat adapt to change, such as the arrival of a new cat in the household.

HOW TO USE RESCUE REMEDY

Rescue Remedy can be used to treat a wide range of different shocks, from the trauma of a major road traffic accident to that of nail clipping. You can also use it in anticipation of a traumatic event, dosing your cat before a trip to the vets, for example. In these situations, start giving it to your cat about forty-five minutes before the anticipated event, giving four drops every fifteen minutes. For use after shocks give four drops every ten to fifteen minutes until your cat appears calmer. For better palatability and acceptance use alcohol-free Rescue Remedy for cats.

Dosage

The dose of Bach flower remedies is four drops at least four times daily. The best way of administering them to your cat is to put them on a little food, such as a treat. Otherwise you can add the four drops to her water bowl and she will get the doses as she drinks throughout the day. It is preferable to offer your cat her doses via a treat, in other words separately from her meal, so that she has a choice in taking the flower remedy. Dosing will be daily for as long as required, but you should review after about three weeks to see how they have helped. Drops should never be administered directly from the dropper into your cat's mouth, as the dropper is made of glass and is hence potentially dangerous. In an emergency

up a bottle of essences ready for you to use. However, if you are consulting books and prescribing the essences for your cat yourself, you will need to buy the stock bottles of each different flower essence that you are using. You then add two drops from the stock bottle of each of your chosen essences (up to a maximum of six different ones), to a 30ml or 50ml bottle of spring water. This bottle of diluted essences is what you will use to dose your cat from. As it is mainly spring water and does not contain any preservative, your bottle of essences will only remain viable for up to three weeks. However, this is the point at which you will be reassessing your cat's progress. At this stage you will either change the combination of flower essences you use, or make her up a new bottle. When preparing and giving the remedies it is important not to touch the tip of the dropper, to avoid contamination.

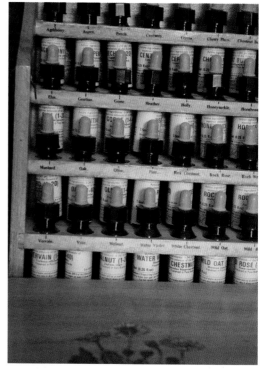

Bach flower remedies are very user-friendly.

situation, when using (alcohol-free) Rescue Remedy, you can give your cat four drops every ten to fifteen minutes. If dosing by mouth is difficult, or if you do not want to give your cat anything to eat, rubbing the drops onto the skin at the base of the ears is another option. They will be absorbed more slowly than if given by mouth, but this is an effective alternative when regular dosing is not possible.

Integrated treatment

Bach flower essences are highly user-friendly and are a great tool for you to use for your cat at home. They are safe and do not have any side effects, and can be used alongside conventional medicines without interference.

How to find a qualified practitioner

A Bach Foundation registered animal practitioner (BFRAP) will be fully qualified to treat emotional and behavioural problems in animals using the Bach flower remedies (*see* Useful Addresses at the back of this book).

TELLINGTON TOUCH

The Tellington Touch or TTouch is a way of healing and training your cat using gentle and directed finger touches anywhere on her body. Your cat can benefit from TTouch to help with a great range of behavioural problems and to enhance health and recovery. Because it is so simple and intuitive TTouch is a popular method of hands-on treatment for cats.

How does it work?

Tellington Touch is a way of working non-habitually with an animal's body to create new behaviour patterns. It works on the understanding that the body's tissues store memories of pain, disease and fear and that the TTouches help to release these, facilitating healing and relaxation. Emotional and mental well-being and balance are intimately linked to physical balance. So, by removing tension in your cat's body by using TTouch, her new, relaxed posture will help her to behave in a calmer and more controlled manner, and hence will help anxious or fearful cats to adapt to new situations. Cats are often treated on a table (less intimidating than standing over them), and sometimes through a towel if they are especially sensitive to touch. TTouch was first developed in the 1970s by the Canadian horse-trainer Linda Tellington-Jones, who based it on the human bodywork therapy called *Feldenkrais*. It involves using repeated, random massage movements on the body to stimulate your cat's nervous system and restore the connections and awareness between mind and body. The understanding is that the brain pays better attention to these unfamiliar sensations and thus TTouch allows change to take place on all levels, from the mental to the physical. The related techniques such as the use of bands and body wraps are an integral part of the TTouch method, and are used to help focus and ground the individual, again achieving the connection between mind and body.

Hands-on healing

Hands-on healing has a history going back thousands of years and has been practised by different cultures all over the world. Holding your hands over a place on that body that hurts is one of our most basic instincts. Thus TTouch is tapping in to this primal instinct to heal. When you use TTouch on your cat you are establishing a non-verbal communication that strengthens the bond between you, and increases trust.

What is it used for?

TTouch is a very effective way of treating a wide range of behavioural and emotional problems. For example, it can be used to calm cats in stressful situations, relieve discomfort and aid healing after surgery or injury, and to help a fearful cat become more confident. TTouch can help to address problems such as noise phobia, separation anxiety and fear. This can be anything from fear of the vet to fear of fireworks or even just the vacuum cleaner. TTouch can also help cats that do not travel well and those who hate being groomed or having their nails clipped. It is also an invaluable aid to training (such as house-training or training not to jump onto kitchen worktops). In addition, it can be used to help stimulate wound healing and in rehabilitation after injury or an operation. TTouch can help to increase circulation, reduce stiffness, promote a feeling of calm and relaxation, change a habitual behaviour, increase self-confidence and release tension.

Your first move – the 'Clouded Leopard'

Cup your hand softly with the thumb and fingers resting lightly on your cat. Use your middle three fingers to make a circular movement as if you are pushing the skin around an imaginary clock-face. Start at the six o'clock position and move the skin in a complete circle and a quarter, clockwise. Small circles are best for cats and the movement should be smooth and flowing. Press just firmly enough to gently slide the skin over the tissues beneath, hold it for a moment and then gently move your hand and repeat this circular TTouch on another area. Avoid making repeated circles on the same spot. This simple TTouch movement is called the 'Clouded Leopard', signifying softness and strength, and you can use it all over your cat's body. Continue for as long as she is enjoying it, paying attention to how she is responding to it at all times. Stop if she moves away, and if she fidgets when you work on a particular part of her body go back to a place where the contact was more acceptable. Your cat may only sit quietly for a few moments to start with, until she gets used to the feeling of TTouch. A variation on the above technique, called the Llama TTouch, where you use the back of your hand, is especially good for anxious cats and those that do not like being touched. It may also be

Tellington Touch helps with healing and relaxation.

a good idea to work through a towel in these individuals, as it minimizes the sensation and helps them to get used to it.

Integrated treatment

One of the major benefits of this form of treatment is that TTouch can be readily learnt and used on your cat every day at home, and you don't need any specialist equipment. It can be used as a complement to any other treatment that your cat is having, or it can be used on its own. It causes no harm, and there are no side effects.

How to find a qualified practitioner

Although the basic techniques can quite easily be learnt, for serious problems you will need the expertise of a trained TTouch practitioner (see Useful Addresses at the back of this book).

CHIROPRACTIC

Chiropractic treatment adjusts misaligned joints throughout the body, paying particular attention to the spine and pelvis. It is based on the philosophy that the spinal column is integral to the health of the whole body due to its relationship with the nervous system. Therefore if the vertebrae are even subtly misaligned they will be putting pressure on the nerves of the spinal cord, and hence having a detrimental effect on the functioning of the entire body. The McTimoney method is a particularly gentle method of chiropractic treatment that is used on animals.

How does it work?

The word chiropractic comes from the Greek word *chiropraktikos*, meaning effective treatment by hand. The McTimoney method was developed by the British chiropractor John McTimoney in the

1950s. It is well suited for use on animals because its gentle nature makes it ethical and respectful. During the treatment the chiropractor will carefully assess the exact orientation of each vertebrae along your cat's spine, and will correct any deviation with very gentle, subtle and extremely quick movements using their fingers. Thus they will work their way along from your cat's head to her tail, correcting and adjusting as they go. Most cats will need a slight adjustment, even if they seem perfectly sound and healthy. By adjusting the misaligned joints throughout the whole body, with special attention to the spine and pelvis, chiropractic treatment can restore health, soundness and normal functioning in a holistic manner. If your cat has been lame or stiff for a while, she may need a few treatments in order for her body to be able to retain the new pattern of alignment. In just the same way that not all cats will tolerate acupuncture, chiropractic manipulation is certainly not applicable to every cat! Some cats find it too invasive and 'hands-on' and will not allow a chiropractor to safely treat them. For such cats it is necessary to look for an alternative method of treatment (perhaps homeopathy or herbalism).

What is it used for?

Your cat can benefit from chiropractic adjustment if she has any back, neck or other musculoskeletal pain or stiffness. This can come about through twisting or jumping or from a fall or other trauma such as a road traffic accident, or she may just be old and arthritic. In addition, because spinal nerves affect all the organs, glands and tissues of the body, chiropractic adjustment has a wider scope of action than simply those affecting your cat's mobility and may be of benefit in problems as diverse as over-grooming or even in cases of chronic urinary tract disease. The aim of chiropractic treatment is to relieve pain and discomfort and increase mobility and flexibility in the body, as well as being a boost to overall health.

Integrated treatment

Your cat may have chiropractic treatment as the sole form of therapy or it may be used in combination with acupuncture or as part of a rehabilitation programme alongside physiotherapy for example. According to chiropractic philosophy, the treatment should be used to maintain health, and not just to treat symptoms. This is why it is best considered as part of a health maintenance regime.

How to find a qualified practitioner

Animal chiropractors can only work by referral from your vet. The McTimoney Chiropractic Association (MCA) was the first, and remains one of the only chiropractic associations to train and qualify chiropractors to treat animals. All animal chiropractors are initially qualified in human chiropractic and do a post-graduate qualification in animal manipulation (see Useful Addresses at the back of this book).

THE LAW AND COMPLEMENTARY THERAPY PRACTITIONERS

According to the Royal College of Veterinary Surgeons' guide to professional conduct, treatment by acupuncture, aromatherapy, homeopathy or any other complementary therapy may only be given by a veterinary surgeon who has undergone training in these procedures. At present, it is illegal for them to be given by practitioners who are not veterinary surgeons. The only exceptions to this that allow non-veterinary surgeons to treat animals are physiotherapists, osteopaths and chiropractors. However, these physical manipulation therapists will still be working under the guidance of a veterinary surgeon, who will refer the animal to them for treatment. You can, however, legally treat your own cat provided you do not cause her 'unnecessary suffering'.

WHAT IS A REFERRAL?

A referral is the process by which your vet sends your cat to a specialist vet, such as one trained in a complementary therapy. A referral will usually be necessary for any of the specialist therapies outlined in this chapter, with the exception of Bach flowers and TTouch which, in some cases, you may practise on your own cat at home. The process of referral generally involves your vet completing a referral form and sending this, together with your cat's full medical history, to the specialist vet. They in turn, send a report back to your vet after the consultation, giving details of the treatment they have prescribed and any other advice concerning your cat's care that they have given. If you request a referral for your cat, your vet is usually obliged to refer you.

2 THE FELINE MIND

Cats are one of the world's most popular pets, with 600 million being kept worldwide. To understand why your cat behaves as she does we need to go back in time and trace her evolutionary journey from the Near Eastern wildcat to today's domestic moggie. That way, by appreciating the forces that shaped her species' behaviour, you will be able to understand what motivates and drives your cat to do what she does – strange as it sometimes seems.

THE EVOLUTIONARY JOURNEY

Genetics reveal that today's domestic cat, *Felis silvestris catus*, is descended from just one of the five subspecies of wildcat that covered the globe from Europe across to Africa and Asia. She is descended from the Near Eastern wildcat, *Felis silvestris lybica*. Her ancestry can be traced back between five thousand and eight thousand years to when man began making settlements, growing crops and storing surplus grain. The African wildcat, a formerly solitary hunter of the savannah, became quite an asset in ancient Egypt, hunting the rats and snakes that feasted in the grain stores. Thus, this became the story of feline domestication, as the wildcats that frequented the grain stores and made themselves useful to man received in exchange food and shelter. It proved a fair exchange and over the next two thousand years the process of domestication evolved and cats became tamer as their association with man developed and grew.

Cats soon spread across the globe, often being taken on sea voyages by sailors and explorers to control rodents on board ship. Indeed, having a cat aboard was considered lucky and fishermen's wives would even keep a black cat at home to prevent disaster at sea. Although the Egyptians prohibited the export of cats, there is no doubt that Phoenician traders transported and traded felines throughout the Mediterranean during this early period. Subsequently, the Roman conquests of Egypt led to the cat spreading throughout the Empire.

Today's cat is descended from the near Eastern wildcat (Felis silvestris lybica).

WORSHIP IN ANCIENT EGYPT

Artefacts from the first millennium BCE show that cats were considered a sacred animal in Ancient Egypt, where they were worshipped as gods. The Egyptian warrior goddess Bastet had the head of a cat and was believed to be their protector. Cats, called *mau*, were often mummified and buried alongside their owners and there is archaeological evidence of 300,000 mummified cats in an Egyptian cemetery. Cats were highly valued animals for pets, vermin control and also as healers. One ancient Egyptian medical text stated that a purring cat would induce a more restful and tranquil night's sleep.

Adaptation and diversity

The evolution of today's domestic cat developed as they moved out from Egypt and found themselves in varying landscapes and climates. As they spread along the trade routes to India and onwards to Burma and Siam, cats found themselves in isolated pockets in the warm and often humid Orient. Here they evolved into the lean, lighter-coloured breeds that came to be classified as Orientals, such as the Burmese and Siamese. Other cats that accompanied traders and travellers east on the silk routes to China became isolated in the cold mountains of Anatolia and Persia (modern-day Turkey and Iran). Here, genetic mutations that led to a long, thick coat and small ears were advantageous and hence we have breeds such as the Turkish Van. Other physical and physiological modifications that occurred as part of domestication included a shrinking of brain size (by up to 25 per cent), because domestic cats no longer had to map and patrol such large territories as their wild ancestors. Similarly, as man protected them, camouflage was no longer crucial to the domesticated cat and their wild, tabby, hunting stripes gave way to an increasing population of solid and bi-coloured individuals.

In contrast to dogs, people have had relatively little influence on cat reproduction; cats have simply gone off and found the mates they favoured. Hence the majority of the cat population today is of no recognized breed and is simply known as either domestic short or domestic long hairs. These cats are also sometimes known as 'moggies' and have coats in colours ranging from ginger to tabby, with every spot and pattern combination in between. Up until the late nineteenth century in Britain most cats were seen as 'just moggies', with looks being unimportant as long as the cat could catch a rat when it needed to. However, at around this time many people were returning from the British colonies, and bringing back with them the local cats that they had adopted there. These imported cats in novel shapes, colours and sizes never seen before in Britain helped to spark the growing interest in pedigree cats and the birth of the 'cat fancy' associations of Victorian times. Cats began to be admired and pedigree cats were bred for their looks, rather than just their mousing ability. The Governing Council of Cat Fancy was founded in 1910 to look after the welfare and keep a register of pedigree cats and there are now over one hundred registered breeds of domestic cat in the UK. Because pedigree cats hail from a smaller gene pool than moggies, they tend to show certain breed specific

SUPERSTITION AND BLACK MAGIC

During the Middle Ages cats were persecuted in Europe. People believed that cats were witches in disguise, linked to paganism and black magic. Many were killed in an effort to ward off evil spirits, so much so that by the end of the fourteenth century the house cat in Britain had almost disappeared. However, in other parts of the world cats have been symbols of good fortune. In Japan the *manekineko* or 'good fortune cat' with its beckoning paw is a well-known talisman of good luck and is present in many shops as a sign of fortuitous business.

Pedigree cats show certain breed specific behaviours.

behaviours. For example, Siamese cats are known for being extrovert in nature and for having a demanding wail-like miaow, whilst Burmese have a reputation for being very affectionate and almost dog-like in their devotion to their owner.

INSIDE THE FELINE MIND

How cats communicate with us and amongst themselves is very much a reflection of their ancestry and their role as solitary hunters. This means that two of the most important aims for every cat are laying claim to territory and keeping out of trouble. Cats much prefer to avoid conflict with their feline neighbours if at all possible (because in the wild injuries through fighting can be life-threatening). That is why they are so adept at communicating (usually through scent) where they have been and where the borders of their territory are. Added to this 'keep out of trouble' mentality, it is also important

when getting inside the feline mind to appreciate that as well as being predators, cats are also a prey species. They would themselves have been hunted by bigger cats in the savannah, and so they are constantly assessing risk and the potential for danger in their surroundings. This is the reason why cats thrive on routine: it gives them a sense of security and makes them feel safe. Cats are solitary hunters and are solitary in much of what they do in their everyday life, from eating to sleeping – they are loners by nature. They are also good at hiding their feelings; it is often difficult to spot stress or anxiety in cats because they have evolved as a species not to show these signs of weakness and vulnerability. In fact cats actually seem to sleep more if they are feeling stressed. This is a form of 'fake sleep', where they appear to be fast asleep but they are really on high alert and can react to the slightest sound, and it can occur in cats that are anxious and on edge in their surroundings.

Territory

Cats are highly territorial creatures and will actively patrol their territory every day (you should look out for your cat making her daily rounds). They defend their patch

Cats are territorial.

because it contains the crucial resources that they need for survival: food, water and shelter. Every cat is different in terms of the amount of territory that they want to call their own. Some will be happy with your (their) home and garden, whilst others want to take on half the neighbourhood and count the garden three doors

Cats love the high life.

down as their boundary (hence, these cats get into more scraps as they fight to defend it). Although cats are generally solitary hunters by nature, in certain circumstances such as bonded family groups it has been seen that related cats can live contentedly together.

The high life

Cats usually love to be able to retreat from the world and observe the goings-on from up high. This is where they feel safest and probably stems from the fact that their wild forebears were great tree climbers. Providing your cat with high-up perches on which to sit and sleep will make her feel more at ease, as will places to hide and retreat, for example providing her with something as simple as a cardboard box.

Nocturnal habits

Cats are crepuscular, which means that they are likely to be most active at dawn and dusk and during the night. Feline vision is adapted to night-time hunting as that is when their prey (the rodent population) is out and about. So don't be surprised if your cat gets up at dawn to leave the house on a hunting trip; that is what she is hard-wired to do! Do be aware, though, that you should not get up and feed your cat during the night if she cries for you. Rewarding this behaviour will create a rod for your own back as she will then cry for attention every night! Instead leave your cat a new plaything or toy out in the evening to keep her occupied at night.

Communication and senses

The first essential skill in cat communication is to see the world as your cat sees it and to appreciate the significance of how she navigates her home and surrounding environments. Get down into all fours and look at your home from your cat's perspective. By understanding how your cat's senses differ from ours, and how important scent is to her, you will begin to be able to appreciate the world from your cat's point of view, and hence learn how you can keep her contented and happy. Cats use a whole repertoire of ways to communicate with us. Look carefully at your cat's eyes, ears, the direction of her whiskers and what she is doing with her tail and body posture, as well as how she uses scent to mark out her territory. Cats are highly tuned in to their surroundings and are easily stressed by certain sights, sounds and scents that are completely undetectable to humans. Vocal communication is far less important for cats than it is for us, but they often learn that humans respond to calls and cries and so they have adapted to use their voices when they want to attract our attention.

Learning to 'speak cat' involves careful observation of signals that can be as subtle as a flick of the tail or a slow blink.

Scent and marking

Cats live in a world where scent is hugely important. They use it to relay information to one another and to mark out their territories and to make themselves feel safe and secure in their environment. Every cat has an individual scent signature that they secrete from special glands on their chin, the corners of their lips, and the top of their head, the base of their tail and between their paws. Cats are so tuned in to the world of scent that they will be acutely aware of even the subtlest changes in the smell of objects and individuals around them. Cats will rub and mark things such as furniture and your legs to deposit their scent and to make these objects feel more familiar. By doing this regularly they are making themselves feel as emotionally safe and secure as possible because their home territory is clearly labelled as theirs. Also be aware that when your cat washes, it isn't just for keeping clean; it is a very important way for cats to coat themselves in their scent as well as to transfer it to their surroundings. So when cats rub themselves on your leg, they are marking you as theirs, rather than just saying 'hello'!

A cat's sense of smell is far more sensitive than ours because they have a highly

Cats live in a world dominated by scent.

FELINE PHEROMONES

Pheromones are naturally occurring scents that animals use to send and receive important information. The feline facial pheromones are chemicals released from glands in the cat's face that are used to mark territory as being safe and secure. It is so effective in modifying a cat's behaviour, helping to keep them calm and relaxed, that it has been synthesized by drug manufacturers and marketed as a spray and a plug-in diffuser.

specialized membrane lining their nose, which can pick up very subtle odours that are undetectable to us. You may also have noticed that your cat curls up her lip when she is sniffing certain odours. The vomeronasal organ in the roof of her mouth enables her to 'taste' certain smells, especially those deposited by other cats. This is called a Flehmen response and is particularly important for entire cats during courtship and mating.

Cats also use urine and faeces as ways to communicate with one another, using a specially concentrated form of urine that they deposit by spraying. Unneutered tomcats routinely spray their urine around their territory to assert their dominance. However, any cat can spray urine and will do so especially when feeling vulnerable or if they perceive a threat to their territory. Sprayed urine is different from the urine passed when cats squat. It is more oily and cats can certainly tell the difference when they sniff it and 'read' the signals from it. In a multiple-cat household spraying is an obvious indicator that all is not well, a sign of turbulent relationships.

Most cats bury their faeces after using the litter tray (or newly dug flowerbed), but where there is a dense feline population they may leave their faeces uncovered and out in the open as a visible territory marker (this is called 'middening').

HOW TO CLEAN OFF URINE SPRAY MARKS

Clean sprayed areas with 10 per cent biological or enzymatic washing powder solution, then rinse thoroughly before drying and spraying with surgical spirit. But don't forget that this is just a symptom that your cat is stressed, and you need to address the cause in order to stop it happening again.

Sight

Cats have difficulty focusing on objects very close to them and focus best at around 2 metres (6ft) away, the zone where they would find their prey. Consequently, when something is placed right under your cat's nose, she will locate it mainly by scent and by vibration and by using her whiskers, rather than by sight. They also have poor detailed vision compared to humans and have comparatively poor colour vision. Cats do not see the same diversity of colours that we do; instead they perceive blues very well, but see yellows, reds and greens as very similar (like people who have a type of red-green colour blindness). What cats do have is amazing night-time vision, suggested to be six times better than ours. This is because they have an extra layer of reflective cells lining the backs of their eyes, allowing them to absorb much more light and see very well in the dark.

WHY DO CATS PURR?

Cats purr when they are happy and content, but also when they are on the vet's table being examined. So always look for the context, as purring doesn't always mean your cat is happy! Kittens purr to attract their mother's attention and she in turn will purr to them when she returns to the nest. Both mother and kittens also purr when she is suckling them. Scientists, however, are still unsure why adult cats purr, although some think that it may be a way of promoting self-assurance and relieving anxiety.

No one knows why cats purr.

Hearing

Cats' ears are ultra mobile and are a very good way of gauging what your cat is telling you. Ears that are tilted forwards mean that your cat is on the alert and listening intently. They can also be flattened right back against her head, usually when she is very frightened. As well as being able to move them around 180 degrees to catch the slightest sound, a cat's ears are able to move independently of each other, so that your cat can be tuned in to several different things at once. The frequency ranges over which cats can hear is much wider than our own, which allows them to detect the minute rustling of rodents in the undergrowth, for example.

Taste

A cat's taste sensations are finely tuned to picking up stale tastes and detecting food that is rancid or past its best. This is an evolutionary adaptation to prevent cats from contracting food-borne diseases from their prey, but nowadays is mostly responsible for cats' finicky feeding habits. Cats commonly, and quite correctly, want food that is fresh at each meal and won't tolerate a tin of food that was opened yesterday for example! Being obligate meat eaters a cat's ability to detect sweetness is limited, concentrating more on bitter, sour and salty flavours.

Touch

A cat's whiskers are a very feline characteristic and are a crucial tool in helping your cat to navigate and understand the world around her. These specialized hairs

A cat's whiskers are vibration and temperature sensitive.

HANDLING YOUR CAT

As a good cat owner, it is important to know what kind of fuss and attention cats enjoy best. As independent animals, cats prefer to 'check in' frequently, with quick strokes or rubs rather than prolonged petting, with some not wanting any physical contact at all. As a rule, cats do not like prolonged periods of fuss and stroking. This means that your cat would usually much prefer that you bend down and offer her a quick stroke many times throughout the day, rather than just one prolonged cuddle or fuss. Sociable cats will usually come and rub around your legs to say 'hello' and then retreat to a vantage place where they can continue to observe, but without contact.

around her face and 'wrists' are vibration and temperature sensitive and help her to see in the dark and to judge distances; they are also useful in indicating your cat's mood. When your cat has her whiskers extended forwards in front of her face, she is concentrating on what's going on, and when they are pulled back tightly against her cheeks this means that she is frightened.

Touch and scent are both used when cats that know each other well greet by touching noses, followed by a full-body rub and ending with a good old nose-to-tail sniff. Adult cats that get along together often groom one another. When they do this they are said to be in the same 'social group' and means, in effect, that they are good friends and enjoy one another's company. By contrast, cats that live together but aren't particular friends appear to be like ships that pass in the night; they tolerate one another's presence but try to have as little physical contact as possible!

Body language
This should always be interpreted in context, based on where your cat is and what's going on at the time. You can't interpret what your cat is saying by looking only at what she is doing with her tail, ears or voice. You need to observe the whole cat, because she communicates with her whole body and you need to put the whole picture together in order to work out what your cat is telling you. Because cats are solitary creatures, they have less need for body language. It's only needed in the main to avoid or to end physical confrontation – as cats would usually do almost anything to avoid a full-blown fight. Visual signalling is very important for cats. They communicate with one another with their eyes, using a slow blink and looking away to show that they are not interested in conflict. Add-

IT'S RUDE TO STARE!

It is often observed that people who say they 'aren't cat people' are the ones that cats make a beeline for! This can be explained by the fact that cats don't like prolonged eye contact. In cat culture being stared at is seen as confrontational. Rivals stare at one another until one backs down and looks away in order to resolve the conflict. People who don't particularly like cats tend not to look at them, which in cat terms is very polite and may be why cats feel more comfortable with these people.

Visual signalling is very important for cats.

ing a yawn to a slow blink emphasizes the message of 'no aggravation', helping to defray any potential fights over territory, for instance.

Another form of visual signalling is the vertical and horizontal scratching that cats do to mark out the boundaries of their territory, such as on tree trunks or fence posts. They have scent glands between their paw pads and so they also leave scent markings when they scratch. This scratching behaviour is also an important way for cats to exercise their leg muscles, flex their claws and sharpen their nails. In order to save your furniture, offer your cat a scratching post instead. Make sure that it is tall enough so that she can get a full stretch when using it. Cats that stand on their tiptoes to leave high scratch marks are advertising how big and strong they are.

A cat's tail has many functions; it acts as a rudder for balance when they are on top of the garden fence, but is also an indicator for their mood and feelings. When taken in the context of their surround-

ings, cats that sweep their tails low from side to side are usually angry and ready for action. If the tip of the tail is twitching then this indicates concentration and interest. A tail held half-lowered or horizontal whilst they are walking along indicates that they are relaxed and confident, whereas if the tail is held straight up with the tip hooked over, this can mean that they are friendly but cautious.

Cats use their tails to communicate their mood.

IS YOUR CAT STRESSED?

Most cats certainly don't appear anxious or upset on the surface because, as a self-reliant species, they have to hide signs of illness, pain or stress in order to survive. Instead, cats communicate that they are stressed and unhappy by their actions, and what they do in their home environment.

Cats can become stressed by certain interactions with people as well as by factors in their environment but by far the greatest area of potential stress is due to other members of their own species. This may be due to having to share their resources and live in close proximity to one or more cats that they don't get on with, or due to the high number of neighbourhood cats resulting in ongoing territorial conflicts.

Signs of stress and unease between members of a multiple-cat household can be subtle. Be on the look-out for warning signs such as turned backs, closed eyes, staring and body blocking. This will usually occur before the spraying, inappropriate elimination and over-grooming that are the more obvious signs that all is not well. Warning signs of tension should never be overlooked in a multiple cat household as the situation won't usually improve or resolve on its own: your cats need your help.

We don't perceive our home in the same way as our cats, so we can often be blind to what may be causing them stress. In human terms providing a loving, warm home where there is always plenty of food down seems the most important factor for keeping our cats happy. But to them living indoors, being bored or having restricted access to resources such as hiding places or litter trays can be very stressful. It is crucial to understand that things that stress your cat can be things

Cats thrive on routine.

SIGNS OF STRESS

Common signs that your cat may be stressed include increased scent marking, scratching on furniture, urine spraying or leaving faeces unburied or in new places or urinating around the house. However, signs of stress can be very subtle and may only be picked up on by noticing changes in your cat's patterns of behaviour. Stressed cats tend to sleep more, change their eating habits (either over-eating or not eating), and they may also groom obsessively, leaving bald patches on their coats.

that you wouldn't find worrying at all. Cats thrive on routine because it makes them feel safe and secure, as they know exactly what's going to happen next. So being predictable in your behaviour and creating daily routines is one easy and helpful stress-buster.

Of course, it is unrealistic to expect that your cat will always have a completely stress-free existence, but by understanding and predicting possible triggers for stress you can at least minimize her exposure to it. This will help to prevent ongoing or chronic stress, which can lead to more serious and complicated behavioural as well as physical complaints.

EVERY CAT IS AN INDIVIDUAL

When all's said and done, despite common feline traits that were inherited from their forebears, every cat is different and has their own unique personality and behavioural repertoire. So, as well as personality differences, a cat's unique temperament will have been shaped, in the main, by how they were brought up as kittens, as well as by how they have experienced life as adults. The most crucial time for the shaping of a cat's future behaviour and temperament is the 'socialization period' between two and seven weeks old. During these few weeks kittens learn all about the world around them from their mother, siblings, people and also other pets. If their experiences during this time are limited, then they may find later life in a busy domestic environment difficult to cope with and be very fearful. Subsequent experiences throughout life will also help to shape a cat's individual temperament and behaviour, based on what they learn happens in any given situation. But it is the early weeks that are the most crucial for a cat's future behaviour and temperament.

Of course, with rescue cats you won't know what kind of experiences they may have been through, but you will have a pretty good idea that they have been negative if your cat is very nervous of everyday encounters. Cats are very quick learners and rapidly make associations in order to avoid repeating negative experiences. This means that it can take several years, if not longer, for very anxious cats to learn to relax in any new environment.

WHAT YOUR CAT WANTS

The link between emotional, mental and physical health is well established in cats, with vets identifying an association between an increasing number of feline ailments and psychological and emotional factors. Your cat's ancestors would have survived by knowing intimately every inch of their territory, monitoring and checking it all the time to make sure that it was safe. In other words, cats are a

Some cats love to play and sleep in simple cardboard boxes!

CAT-FRIENDLY LIVING

- Cats live in a world of scent, so be aware of how your clothes and bags can carry strange scents into the house and how anything that alters the scent profile of your home can affect your cat's awareness of their territory.
- Two's company, three's a crowd. It is preferable to have only one or two cats in a household, as they are solitary creatures and highly territorial.
- Cats are most active at dawn and dusk and are active night-time hunters by nature.
- Cats like to eat and drink in separate locations and need to have their bowls scrupulously clean.
- Cats like to play, whatever their age.
- Staring is rude. Cats do not like prolonged eye contact but can be made more at ease if you give them a slow blink.
- Make sure that visitors allow your cat to make the first move and let them come up for attention if and when they want it.
- Cats feel safer when they are up high – give them plenty of opportunity to go somewhere high up to retreat to.
- Make any changes gradually, as cats love routine and like to know where everything is.

species that need to feel they are in control of their environment. You can help your cat to do this at home by offering her a variety of places to hide and feel safe. That way, if circumstances become stressful for her, she has a choice of safe spots to retreat to. Similarly, you can increase your cat's sense of security by making sure that everything in her world is predictable; so avoid making any sudden changes to room layout or household make-up (new pets, people, and so on). Your cat thrives on routine and knowing that everything in her territory is in the right place. Next, make sure that your cat has plenty of new and interesting things to do, such as toys that she likes to play with or areas to climb and explore. Even older cats thrive when they are mentally as well as physically engaged and fulfilled. Finally, take the time to try to understand your cat's unique personality and preferences, and what sort of contact or interaction she enjoys, remembering that less is often more when it comes to felines.

On look-out in the garden.

MAKING YOUR HOME CAT-FRIENDLY

Now you know all about how cats perceive the world and what's most important to them, you can put this into practice in making your home an oasis of feline comfort. A cat-friendly home will firstly not have too many cats in it! As cats are by nature solitary types, a one-cat household is often preferable, especially if the surrounding neighbourhood has a high cat density. If you are looking to have two cats then siblings or littermates are the most likely to get along (*see* Chapter 3).

You need to think about what your home is like from your cat's point of view. Get down on all fours again and have a look around you. Try to imagine how daunting certain areas of your home might be to your cat. Are there places where she could feel trapped, or perhaps too exposed, with nowhere to hide? Create plenty of hideaways, such as boxes, tunnels, cupboards and spaces under beds or on top of wardrobes to which your cat can retreat and feel safe (remembering that cats usually feel safer up high). Cats love to hunt and chase, so having areas in the house such as corridors and long hallways where you can play games with your cat is a great idea. Providing climbing frames and activity centres for your cat (especially indoor cats) will really help to engage her and give her a rewarding and interesting way to amuse herself and keep mentally as well as physically agile.

Everyone knows that a cat's number one daily activity is sleeping. So providing your cat with plenty of choices of cosy bed is another must in the feline-friendly home. Be creative with the different types of bed (those like an igloo, or radiator beds for instance), and the location – you'll soon get to know what kind of nest your cat prefers. Most cats are born sun-bathers so may like a bed on a sunny windowsill, whilst others prefer to be next to a heater, or in a cooler spot with fresh air, depending on whether they have a long or short coat and what kind of temperature they prefer. Get your cat a dedicated scratching post to save your expensive leather sofa from being destroyed. But be aware that your cat won't use it unless it is positioned in the right place, and is tall enough. To begin with put it in a place where you have noticed that your cat tends to hang out a lot and where she appears to be most at ease, though you may have to move it if your cat doesn't use it here. The ideal scratching post needs to be tall enough so that your cat can stretch out to her full height when using it, and be secure enough that it doesn't tip over or feel wobbly. Although the majority of cats perform vertical scratching (also called 'stropping'), some prefer to do it horizontally, in which case your carpet may suffer!

Next, think about providing adequate litter trays for your cat. Even if your cat has access to the outdoors there may be times when she needs to use a litter tray in the house (such as if she is unwell or if she is afraid to go outside), so it is important that there is always one available in case. If you have more than one cat you will need to have several litter trays, as this is a resource that can cause tension between cats if it is in short supply. Be aware that the type of litter tray (such as whether it has a roof on) and its location in the house, as well as the type of litter itself (texture, odour and composition), will have an effect on how keen your cat will be to use it. Keeping litter trays reg-ularly cleaned out will be important for your cat's comfort.

Finally, be aware of how scrupulously clean cats are when it comes to eating and drinking. In their natural habitat they would never eat and drink from the same location so that there would be no risk of water contamination. Mirror this at home by keeping your cat's food and water bowls thoroughly clean, and by keeping the bowls well apart (avoid those double bowls where food and water are right next to one another).

HELP FOR ANXIOUS CATS

Some cats are anxious and timid by nature; others have had traumatic experiences in life and have ended up having many fears. Whatever the reason, there are many ways that you can help an anxious cat to feel more comfortable and relaxed. Providing plenty of places for your cat to retreat to and hide in is important. These can be as simple as cardboard boxes placed up on top of a cupboard, or providing a cushion in the bottom of the wardrobe and leaving the door ajar so that your cat can creep in and hide if she feels overwhelmed. You can also use a calming aid such as Dr Bach's Rescue Remedy (two to four drops added to a treat), or a plug-in diffuser pheromone product (*see* 'Feline pheromones' box, earlier in this chapter) which can help to relieve stress and anxiety. Finally, ensure that you keep to as much of a routine as possible and make any changes to the furniture or room layout very gradually – cats feel most secure when everything around them is familiar.

3 MULTIPLE-CAT HOUSEHOLDS

With the link between physical, mental and emotional health now well established, vets are seeing an increasing number of feline ailments where psychological and emotional factors play a significant role.

One of the principal factors contributing to the stress and emotional anxiety of so many of our cats today is the fact that they have to live in 'multiple-cat households'. This is exacerbated by the fact that because cats are such popular city pets, there is often a high density of neighbourhood cats to contend with too. This situation has been largely created by the fact that many cat owners love to have more than one cat (often adopting several), and the idea that cats are good pets for life in the city. Sadly, the paradox is that cats themselves often find it difficult living in groups and also need a good amount of space around them to call their own.

Having more than one cat in a household can be problematic because by their very nature cats are solitary creatures. Most regular-sized households simply aren't big enough to provide the core territory and easy access to resources for more than one or two cats. This is a cause for concern because where access to food and litter trays, for example, is limited, anxiety and stress can result. And limited access does not just mean that you haven't put down enough litter trays or food bowls, it also means that your cat may find it difficult and stressful to get to them if they have to pass close to one or more feline housemates on the way. There simply isn't enough room for more

Relationships between cats are complex.

than one, or at a push two, cats in most human households – we just can't accommodate the size of territory a cat usually prefers to call their own.

Relationships between cats are complex. Whether a cat views another cat as a friend, an adversary or a rival depends very much on whether they are related, as well as when and how they were first introduced to one another and what their current circumstances are. In this chapter we will investigate the best way to integrate cats and other pets together into a household and how to minimize potential stress and anxiety in multiple-cat households.

TERRITORY AND RESOURCES

Having more than one cat in a territory as small as the size of a regular human home will be a cause of stress and anxiety for most cats. A cat's territory consists of a 'core area' where they feel secure enough to eat, sleep and play, and it is this hub that your cat will actively defend and call her own. Extending from this core area is your cat's hunting range, usually not more than a few hundred metres, where they may roam and patrol on a regular basis.

A relaxed cat who lives on her own.

Cats rely on their home environment to provide them with their 'resources', which consist of food, water, comfort, protection and security. Anything that threatens their resources causes stress, and the most common threat that they perceive will be in the form of another cat in their home.

Before getting more than one cat it pays to think about the size of your home and also the number of cats that are already in your neighbourhood. These factors will make a big difference to the number of cats that you can happily accommodate. If there is already a significant resident cat population in your area then this may well represent additional pressure on territory for your new cat. So you may need to think again about whether it would be wise to have more than one.

Independent nature
This is one of a cat's most notable personality traits and is often why people choose them as pets. It is due to this innate, independent nature that cats rely much more on their surroundings to keep themselves happy than on the presence of other individuals around them. As they are not a social species (like dogs and humans) the majority of cats are more content to be on their own, as long as their environment satisfies their general needs. What every cat requires in order to live contentedly is easy access to plentiful 'resources'. These include food and water, as well as a litter tray (or toilet area outside), a scratching post, high up resting places and nice, cosy, hidden dens to which they can retreat.

In multiple-cat households there will undoubtedly be tension and stress over shared resources because the presence of other cats is perceived by each individual to mean that their precious resources are under threat. Every cat feels safest and most content when they are in control of their own territory (your house). This usually happens when they are the only cat in it and so have total control over access to their food, water, litter tray or bed. Appreciating these factors will help us to understand why behavioural and physical complaints linked to stress occur more frequently in multiple-cat homes, and what we can do about it.

Always bear in mind that there may be plenty of room and opportunity to access their resources in a stress-free manner if there are just two cats in the household. However, problems usually arise when there is a third or even a fourth cat in the home as this causes them to be just too close for comfort, with too many potential sources of conflict and competition.

Feline relationships

Feline relationships are complicated and can change over time, just as human relationships do. Some cats form strong bonds with certain individuals rather than others; in other words, cats choose their own friends. Whether cats are likely to get along with one another can be linked to factors such as whether they are related to one another, what sex and age they are and how they were initially introduced, but it is also down to individual compatibility and personality.

Cats naturally bond with their mother and siblings, so if you are considering whether to have more than one cat think about the benefits of getting littermates of opposite sexes (there will be less sibling rivalry). Siblings usually get along better than unrelated individuals. Although they usually play together and are very close as kittens, they become more independent, but still closely bonded, as they get older.

People often think that unrelated cats, introduced to one another as adults, will

Cats are independent by nature.

become friends and enjoy each other's company. However, it is much more likely that they will remain as individuals living independently from one another, in the same area. In other words, they are not friends, they are just co-existing within the same living space. If you watch cats who live like this it becomes clear that they tend to occupy their own separate areas of the house and time-share communal spaces so that they have as little close contact as possible. Hence it will be extra stressful for these cats if they are shut in the same room together when you are out, for example. Equally, feeding time can become a source of anxiety if both cats are fed next to one another as this can create tension around competition for food. This is why it is preferable to have several feeding stations in different parts of the house and to provide free access kibble during the day in the various feeding stations, so as to avoid any potential conflict.

However much you wish your cats would be best buddies, never force them to sit next to one another or cuddle up together as this can be highly stressful for them. Equally, if they have to pass each other in a corridor or hallway in order to get to the litter tray or cat-flap, for example, this too can be a source of everyday stress. As with the feeding stations, ensure there are sufficient litter trays in different parts of the house, working on the 'one each, plus one extra' principle. This will make it easier for each cat to feel more comfortable at home. Carefully observe your cats at home and work out who likes to hang out where in both the house and the garden, and then make sure that you have duplicate sets of everything in each area. This means that they can then access their resources whenever they choose, without having to come into contact or pass too close to another cat – a recipe for a happy feline family. Remember, choice helps to give your cats a sense of control and being in control is what they thrive on.

Cats that are 'friends' with one another and are said to be bonded companions sometimes rub against one another with their heads, flanks and tails. They may also groom one another, especially after a spat, when mutual grooming can help cats to calm down and restore harmony to their relationship.

Visiting the vet

This has a special mention for multiple-cat households because particular problems can arise when you have to take one of the clan to the vets. If one cat comes home smelling 'vetty', the other residents may gang up on them as they smell unfamiliar and unlike part of the 'home' group. (It is also possible that the smell of the vets can evoke bad memories in the other cats, which adds to their hostile reaction). You can help to prevent such circumstances by wiping the patient with a cloth before she

This cat's favourite bed is just a box!

leaves home and then wiping her again with the same cloth, to renew her normal scent, before she gets home. Always supervise reintroductions carefully when you bring one cat home from the vets (or any other strange environment) and be ready to provide a distraction with toys if tensions develop. If one cat is away at the vets for a prolonged stay then it may be necessary to take the same steps to reintroduce them to the group as you do for a brand new housemate (*see below* 'feline decorum').

COMMON PROBLEMS IN MULTIPLE-CAT HOUSEHOLDS

Urine spraying

Urine spraying is a form of territorial marking behaviour. Cats do this for one of two reasons; most commonly it is a sign that they are feeling stressed and vulnerable and need to reassert their position as owner of their territory, but highly confident cats may also do it to assert their dominance. In a multiple-cat household spraying indoors is a sure sign that one or more of the cats doesn't feel secure in their home and that they are stressed. Studies have shown that the likelihood of urine spraying increases in direct proportion to the number of cats within a household. Spraying is far more common in unneutered animals, and is more common in males than females. Neutered cats may also spray urine, but this is not common.

Sprayed urine is different from the urine cats pass when they squat in the litter tray; it is oilier and smellier, and is passed in much smaller amounts. Cats usually spray urine at the boundaries or entry/exit points to their territory and when they do this outside it is actually part of their normal behavioural repertoire. It's when your cat starts spraying *inside* that you have a problem.

HOW TO RECOGNIZE SPRAYING BEHAVIOUR

A cat that is going to spray will first sniff the area closely (it is usually a vertical surface, such as a wall or fence), and then back up towards it; then, holding the tail up straight and quivering, he urinates. There is usually only a very small amount of urine, so it can be difficult to see; you may instead smell it.

House soiling

Cats are well known for being highly fastidious creatures and usually prefer to use their litter tray or favoured spot in the garden for toileting. Thus finding urine or faeces in your home can be a sign that something is wrong and that your cat may well be stressed or have a medical complaint. Occasionally, of course, one-off accidents can happen, for example if your cat couldn't get to the litter tray or if there was no litter tray available. However, if your cat is soiling outside her litter tray on a regular basis, then this is usually a sign of stress or that she is unwell, and in either case she needs to be checked over by the vet.

Cats can urinate inappropriately in the house as well as spray urine, but these are two different behaviours and it is important to be able to differentiate between them. This is because they have different causes and different solutions. Spraying (as described in the box above) is most commonly a stress-related reaction, whereas if your cat is squatting to

45

Litter trays are an important resource.

Once your cat has urinated or defecated once in a particular (inappropriate) location in your home, they will be more inclined to use this area as their regular toilet due to the scent marks they have left. This is why cleaning the area quickly is important, as is keeping your cat away from it for a while afterwards in order to help prevent any bad habits from forming.

There are many different reasons why cats may soil indoors, ranging from their litter tray not having been cleaned out to having the wrong type of litter in it, as well as whether it has a scent. Cats can be very fussy when it comes to their personal habits. Most cats don't like to use a litter tray if it is soiled, so lack of regular or thorough cleaning can be a potential cause of inappropriate soiling in the house. Changing the consistency or type of litter you use can all affect your cat as they have such a keen sense of smell and some strong odours can be very unpleasant for them. It may be as simple as a change in the type of litter used that has created enough anxiety in your cat to cause them to defecate or urinate in

urinate in inappropriate areas around the house it is likely to be linked to a painful medical complaint such as cystitis (although this may also be purely a behavioural problem).

To urinate, a cat squats and voids urine onto a horizontal surface and may then scratch around the area. Common sites of inappropriate urination include sofas, carpets, duvets and sinks, but it can occur in any location. To spray, on the other hand, cats back up towards a vertical surface, tail straight up and quivering, and jet a small volume of smelly, oily urine onto the wall. Common sites for spraying include window and door frames, around the cat-flap and on shopping bags.

WHY DO CATS URINATE ON THEIR OWNERS' BEDS?

Their owner's bed is not an uncommon place for cats to urinate or even defecate. This spot is chosen not out of spite or as a 'dirty protest', but because it is the place in the home where many cats feel most safe and secure. When they are urinating or defecating cats are at their most vulnerable, hence they choose their owner's bed as the safest spot they know.

Over-grooming can be caused by stress.

the house. Where you position the litter tray will also have an effect on whether your cat will like to use it. Place it in a quiet location, well away from your cat's food and water stations and away from noisy household objects (such as washing machines). It is also worth bearing in mind that some cats prefer covered litter trays, as this makes them feel less vulnerable.

Finally, a vet check-up is always warranted for any cat that exhibits inappropriate urination or house soiling because it may be due to a medical complaint that requires treatment, such as a urinary tract infection or diarrhoea.

Over-grooming

Over-grooming refers to any behaviour that goes beyond what your cat needs to do on a daily basis to maintain her coat and to distribute her scent over her body. Symptoms of over-grooming include patches of hair loss where there may be broken hair shafts that feel rough and spiky. (This can help the vet to distinguish over-grooming from conditions of alopecia where the remaining hair in the area feels normal and soft to the touch.) Over-grooming can occur on any part of the body that your cat can reach with her tongue, but commonly it affects the inside of the legs, the belly and the flanks.

Although over-grooming can initially be linked to pain or irritation of the skin, it is widely agreed that stress also plays a significant role. Cats often groom themselves to make themselves feel better when they are anxious or in a stressful situation. This can then turn into a compulsive behaviour that they then do all the time. As with any worrying symptom or behaviour always consult your vet so that they can help to diagnose the problem correctly, because over-grooming can be confused with skin conditions such as allergies that may require medical treatment.

MANAGING MULTIPLE-CAT HOUSEHOLDS

To make your home into the best possible place for more than one cat to happily

Cats usually prefer to live on their own.

of sleeping spots, make sure that there are plenty of high up places available, as well as hidden-away quiet retreats for your cats to rest in. Provide several tall scratching posts and make sure that your cats have easy access to the outdoors via a cat-flap.

Combine your knowledge of what every feline needs with what you know about each cat's individual preferences and personalities, to equip your home for them in the best possible way. Taking account of their ancestral inheritance as solitary hunters, their individual natures and also your cats' learned behaviours and responses will all be factors in how you arrange your home to suit them best. Timid cats will benefit from more hideaways and places to retreat to.

In essence, for a harmonious feline household ensure that all resources (beds, food and water bowls, scratch posts, litter trays, high places to sit, hiding places and toys) are provided according to the principle of 'one for each cat plus one extra'.

Ultimately, if you have all of the elements in place to create the best possible environment for your cats but there are still problems, then it can be a good idea to call in a specialist cat behaviour expert. Investigating the feline politics in

co-habit you'll need to ensure that it has enough 'resources' for each one of your cats. This means providing one litter tray for each cat, plus one extra. Make sure that these are placed in different locations around the house, one on each floor, so that each cat can easily access them without coming into conflict with a feline housemate. You will also need to offer individual food and water bowls for each cat placed in different areas around the kitchen, again so that there is less potential for stress or competition at feeding time. In multiple-cat homes it is also a good idea to leave dry food out for your cats as they can then graze in their own time throughout the day. In terms

---

COLLAR-ACTIVATED CAT-FLAPS

To stop the added anxieties of uninvited guests entering your cats' home, fit a microchip- or collar-activated cat-flap so that only they can use it. This is a great way of helping to keep your feline home environment as safe and secure as possible and is especially valuable for multiple-cat households.

---

a multiple-cat home is complicated and professional behaviourists will be able to spot the subtle signs that are easy to miss and can help you solve your 'multiple-cat' problem.

FELINE DECORUM – HOW (SOME) CATS CAN LEARN TO GET ALONG

There are no hard and fast rules about how to choose a new cat to bring into a resident cat's home, but some authorities claim that one of the opposite gender, neutered and younger than the resident, makes for a good choice.

The first thing to do when you bring a new cat home is to settle her in and provide her with a safe sanctuary, a quiet place with everything that she needs: beds, food and water, a litter tray, a scratching post, places to hide away and toys. This room or area should not be freely accessible to the other cats in the household, as it is your new cat's special den where she is going to take time to settle in to her new home.

First impressions count

It is commonly said that people make up their minds about whether they like someone within the first few moments of meeting them, and it is not so different for cats. They too can make quick judgements about whether or not they are inclined to get along with another cat or not. This means that the first impression that your resident cat has of their potential new housemate is of crucial importance as to whether they will hit it off. Fearful or aggressive first encounters can set up patterns of behaviour between the two cats that can be very difficult to break. So bringing your new cat home and just 'letting them get on with it' in terms of meeting your resident feline just

won't work and is in fact a recipe for disaster. The best way of managing a careful and hopefully amicable introduction between two cats is to take things very slowly.

Cats need the right environment for meeting their potential new friend, where they have time and space and where they can perform their proper social greetings correctly. Bear in mind that there aren't many cats who would instantly welcome a newcomer into their territory and just sit back and offer them the best armchair!

The first thing to do is allow each cat to have access to the other's scent, well before they have face-to-face introductions. This way you can keep each cat in a separate part of the house to begin with and just let them get used to one another's presence via their scent, while they are still feeling safe in their areas. You can achieve this scent swapping by taking each cat into the other's room (when they are not there), and playing with them and allowing them to leave their scent markings. The next step in the process will be to start to produce a 'household scent' pattern, by stroking one cat and then going to the other and stroking them, and vice versa. This will allow both cats' individual scents to mingle and produce one 'household' scent that may help them bond as one unit and recognize one another as friends, not foes, at a later stage of the introduction process.

Brief encounters

Putting the new cat into a confined area such as a crate (borrowing a puppy crate can be a good idea) or cat basket and then allowing the resident cat into the room for a short period of time to meet her is usually the next step of the introductory process. Make sure that the pen or carrier for the new cat is big enough,

Comfy beds are another important resource.

reduce feelings of anxiety and confrontation between the cats.

At this stage your cats should still be kept separate from one another whilst you can't supervise them. During each one of their short introductory sessions observe the cats closely, looking out for what their body language is telling you. Look at the position of their tails, where they are looking, how frequently they are scent marking and whether they are becoming more relaxed in one another's company. As part of this introductory phase you may also find it helpful to put your resident cat into the carrier whilst your new inhabitant has the chance to roam around and get to know her new home without trouble.

Once you are happy that things are progressing well you can start to feed them at opposite ends of the room (with the new cat still in her pen/carrier), but over time (usually a few days to a week) you can work towards feeding them closer together.

and has a place where she can retreat and hide, so that the resident cat doesn't intimidate her. Equally, make sure that the resident cat has an escape route too; leave the door open so that they can get away when they've had enough. Never force introductions and keep the meeting time brief to begin with as little and often is much more advantageous than prolonged exposure where either cat can become distressed.

It is also important that you don't put the cats into a position where they have to make eye contact with one another when they are summing each other up (remember that cats feel intimidated if they are stared at). Place the cat carrier or crate somewhere above ground level, such as on a table, and this will help

INTRODUCTION TIPS

Familiarity breeds contentment as far as cats are concerned, so do all that you can to ensure that your new cat's and your resident cat's scents are mingled so that they smell familiar to one another when they meet. As well as stroking one cat and then the other, you can also accelerate the spread of 'family scent' by wiping a soft cloth around the cheeks and mouth of your new cat and then wiping this around your furniture (at cat head height), concentrating on doorways, and also wiping it on other pets.

D-Day

After all this preparation you can't put D-Day off any longer and it will be time to allow these two cats to get to know one another for real. Their first proper meetings should always be supervised and there should always be plenty of exit routes and places to retreat to and hide, so that either cat can get away if it all gets too much.

Do remember, though, that despite all your best intentions and careful introductions, personality differences play a huge role in all social interactions and resulting friendships, and some cats, just like some people, simply don't get along.

ARE DOGS AND CATS COMPATIBLE HOUSEMATES?

Generally speaking, it is said that cats tend to get on with dogs better than they do with other cats. This may be because dogs are not seen as competition for territory or food. It is also sometimes said that it is easier to introduce a dog into a household with a resident cat, than vice versa. If either the cat or the dog is rescued, then of course there is the possibility that they have co-habited with the other species before. This may have been a happy experience, or it may not. With luck the rescue centre will have given you some indication as to whether it is possible for your pet to live with the other species in question.

One of the keys to successful pairing of feline and canine companions, just as when new cats first meet one another, is a careful and well-planned introduction. Consideration of the following will be important: compatibility of age, sex, breed, size, character and training. The breed of dog will usually have a significant impact on how they behave with a cat; terriers and greyhounds (and some other breeds) were bred to chase, and a cat will almost certainly seem like fair game, at least at first. Equally, puppies or young dogs will probably be more excitable and ready to chase and play, which is not a behaviour most cats will appreciate.

Finally, don't forget that cats and dogs use a different language (think about what a wagging tail may mean to either species), and that most dogs will find it difficult to suppress a chase instinct if a cat runs away from them.

Cross-species introductions

The basis of an introduction between cats and dogs is basically the same as the programme for introducing two cats. Keep them in separate parts of the house to begin with and use their unique scents as a means of letting each of them know that they have a new companion nearby. Do this by stroking each of them separately without washing your hands in-between, so that they can each smell one another's scent and it will be familiar when they meet for the first time.

For the first meeting, it is a good idea to have the cat in either a pen or a travelling cage so that they feel secure and protected. Place this above the dog's eye level. It is also a good idea to have walked your dog beforehand so that he is less energetic. Have him on the lead and ask him to sit quietly, making sure that you quickly reward calm interaction (in other words just looking and staying quiet and calm), with the cat. Never put them too close to one another or force any contact. Again, as with the cats, short, frequent, controlled meetings are best. Most dogs settle down once they realize that the cat isn't actually that interesting and isn't always going to play and chase!

A two-species household.

There is no hard and fast rule about how long it will take your pets to get to know one another or how long it should be before you dispense with the pen/ cage and allow free interaction. It may be a week or a few weeks. However, do make sure that you keep your dog on the lead when they are together until you are happy that they get along. Always make sure that each (the cat especially) has the opportunity to escape and has their own 'safe zones' to take refuge in.

A HELPING HAND

If you do want some extra help for those first introductions there are a few ways to do it. First of all there is Dr Bach's Rescue Remedy. A few drops of this in both animals' water bowls for the week of the introduction will help relieve any anxiety or panic in both parties. You may also choose to use the Bach flower remedy 'Walnut' as this helps pets 'adapt to changes'. A new pet is certainly a change and will take some getting used to. And don't forget the synthetic pheromone products that are available from your vets (DAP and 'Feliway'), which can be useful in helping to smooth the transition period.

Co-habitation

Once the introductions have been made and you have a multiple-species household, make sure that your cat or cats have places to eat, sleep and 'use the toilet' that are well out of the dog's way. For example, beds should be placed where the dog can't reach them, such as on the top of the wardrobe, and their food and water bowls should be high up and out of his reach. Finally, don't forget to make sure that the litter tray is somewhere quiet and dog-proof.

The successful cat–dog household is one where the dog has a healthy respect for his feline companion (usually brought about by a few carefully aimed swipes from the cat), and leaves her well alone.

4 THE KITTEN

There is no doubt that having a new kitten is great fun and a real joy. But they need a lot of patience and it can be a time-consuming job to set the house rules and get them litter trained! The main developmental stages of a kitten's early life take only a few short weeks but have a lasting effect on the mental and physical characteristics of the adult cat they become. So, kitten-hood is an important time to make sure that your new friend is exposed to all the sights, sounds and experiences that they need to be accustomed to as adults.

This chapter introduces kitten care from birth right through to adulthood, concentrating on how to feed and care for them and explaining the importance of socialization and play to a kitten's mental and physical development. (Vaccination, worming and neutering are covered in Chapter 8.)

PREGNANCY AND BIRTH

Cats reach sexual maturity and are able to breed from around six months old. If female cats have not been neutered by this age and are let outside, then there is a strong possibility that the local tomcat will find them and before you know it you've got a pregnant queen. ('Queen' is the term used to describe a female cat that is used for breeding.)

Pregnancy in cats lasts sixty-three days (around nine weeks), and because sexual activity in the females is linked to day length, most litters are born in the spring and summer months. During the first few weeks of pregnancy there is very little outward change, but you may notice your cat's nipples becoming pinker and more visible. She will then gradually begin to fill out as the kittens develop and in the days before the birth she will begin to produce milk. She will usually show nesting behaviour about two weeks prior to giving birth as she searches for a safe and warm place to have her litter. You can help by providing her with a cardboard box or drawer, but she will more than likely choose her own favoured spot, sometimes in the laundry cupboard or even on your bed! Most cats give birth easily, without the need for any human intervention. The queen will lick each kitten as soon as they are born, to help stimulate them to breathe and begin to suckle (she also ingests the placentas).

Every kitten's development begins in the womb, so the queen's diet and health

Your new kitten.

during pregnancy have a significant effect on that of her offspring. Although every cat is different, as a general guide it is suggested that the amount of food she receives during pregnancy should be gradually increased from the second week of gestation so that by the time she is giving birth the queen is being fed between 25 and 50 per cent more than normal. However, because most cats adapt well to free choice feeding (leaving food down for her), this is often the best way to provide the pregnant queen with adequate nutrition.

Finally, despite it being a popular choice to keep one of your cat's offspring rather than finding homes for all the kittens, this really isn't necessary for the mother. She will get along very well once her kittens are weaned and will adjust easily to being on her own again.

THE EARLY DAYS

Kittens are born with their eyes closed and their ears folded over, so a newborn kitten is really defenceless, being both blind and deaf to begin with. Their mother will help them to feed by licking them and helping them to locate the milk. She will also purr as her kittens suckle, and the vibration that this creates helps the newborn kittens to find her.

Kittens have a rapid growth rate and by the end of their first week will already have doubled in weight, tripling their birth weight by the time they are three weeks old. To sustain such a good growth rate kittens spend much of their first few weeks simply suckling. They help maintain the flow of milk by kneading their mother's stomach with their paws (a habit some cats retain as a comforting activity in adulthood). They remain highly dependent on their mum for these early weeks, relying on her for everything from feeding, cleaning, defecating (she licks each kitten's bottom after they have fed to stimulate them to defecate), and for keeping warm.

Although suckling milk for nourishment is required for only five to six weeks, it usu-

Kittens suckle soon after birth.

ally continues for the emotional benefits it provides for at least as long again, right up until the mother begins the weaning process. Kittens quickly start to become self-sufficient and are capable of fully grooming themselves by about five weeks old. Their eyes usually open at around one to two weeks of age and their ears will also have developed by this stage, so that they can now hear properly. It is true, however, that in some breeds, such as the Siamese and Orientals, kittens' eyes can open from as early as a few days old.

When the kittens are about four weeks old, the mother gradually begins to wean them off her milk and on to solid food. So, if all goes to plan, you don't have to do much in terms of kitten care for the first few weeks, apart from making sure that the mother cat is healthy and well fed.

Hand-rearing is very time-consuming.

HAND-REARING

Occasionally, however, kittens have to be hand-reared, either because their mother is unwell or has died, or because she has rejected them. (Queens can reject their offspring especially if they are unwell or have a serious health problem that makes them less likely to survive.) Sometimes kittens from very large litters may also need to be hand-reared because their mother simply can't feed her whole brood.

Helping to raise an orphaned kitten can be a very rewarding experience, as well as being hard work. Depending on the circumstances, it can mean feeding the kittens for a few days if their mother is ill, some supplementary feeding for a large litter, or it may mean hand-feeding right up until weaning.

The most basic needs of kittens in the majority of hand-rearing situations will include the provision of a safe, comfortable, clean and warm environment. Added

to this you will have to provide a suitable feeding regime, usually every few hours for the first three weeks. Newborn kittens need up to ten feeds in every twenty-four-hour period. So, like babies, kittens need to be with their carer at all times so that you can keep an eye on them. This

---

MILK REPLACEMENT AND FEEDING TIMES

It is important to use only a properly formulated replacement queen's milk for hand-reared kittens. This is available from veterinary practices or pet shops. Cow or goat's milk should not be used because the protein and fat levels are much too low. As a guide, most kittens less than two weeks old will need feeding every two hours; between two and four weeks this can be extended to every two and a half to three hours, and at four to five weeks old, five to six feeds a day is usually adequate. Always ask your vet for detailed advice on hand-rearing.

HELPING KITTENS TO URINATE AND PASS MOTIONS

In their first two weeks of life kittens rely on their mother's help in order to be able to go to the loo. She will lick their bottoms after they have suckled, and this stimulates their 'voiding reflex' by which urine and faeces are released. In hand-reared kittens, where the mother is not available to do this job, it is up to you to play this role until weaning. You can do this by using a clean, damp cloth, gently stimulating their ano-genital area both before and after feeding.

means that many changes in lifestyle may be needed if you have taken on the hand-rearing of one or more kittens. In their first few weeks you will also have to take over the mother's role in helping the kittens to empty their bowels and to urinate (*see* box).

The final word should be that hand-rearing is very time-consuming, requires expertise and is not always successful, so should never be taken on lightly or without seeking professional guidance on how to do it properly. If you do find yourself in the situation of having to care for orphaned or abandoned kittens, always ask your local vet for help and advice about hand-rearing.

YOUR NEW KITTEN

Kittens are usually ready to go to their new home from around eight to nine weeks old, although there is some debate about the most suitable age. Some authorities advocate leaving kittens with their mother until around twelve weeks so that they have more time for suckling and social development with their family. Pedigree kittens normally stay with their mother for slightly longer and aren't ready to go until around thirteen weeks old (by which stage they are usually fully vaccinated). In all events, as long as your new kitten is over eight weeks old, is weaned and appears to be happy and healthy, they are usually ready to go to their new home.

Before you get your new kitten it pays to consider what kind of cat you would like to own: short or long haired, moggie or purebred pedigree? The choice of coat length is important because long-haired cats definitely need more attention to grooming and need to learn to be brushed regularly, from an early age. Purebred or pedigree cats are often chosen for their looks or because of their particular character traits. This is because pedigree cats tend to show particular characteristics associated with their more limited genetic blueprint. Certain breeds such as the Orientals (for example, the Siamese cat) are known for being particularly vocal, and others, such as the Burmese, for being very affectionate and faithful. So it is important to study your chosen pedigree's breed profile, or better still go and meet cats of the type before you take the plunge. As for gender, most cats are neutered so this will usually be a less important decision, unless of course you plan to breed from them.

However, having said all this, by far the most likely circumstance is that you will pay a visit to your local cat rescue centre and come home with whichever kitty caught your eye! Re-homing a kitten, as opposed to an adult cat, usually allows you to be able to mould their behaviour patterns to fit in with your lifestyle, and

Kittens are usually ready to go to their new home at eight to nine weeks old.

hence make life easier. Added to this, kittens are undoubtedly great fun to have around and you will enjoy watching as well as participating in all their playful antics as they grow up.

Bringing your new kitten home – the first night

There will be a lot for your kitten to adjust to when she arrives at her new home with you. You can take a few simple steps to help her to adjust and to feel at home, such as by providing her with a familiar object (a blanket or toy) from her previous home. You can also help your kitten to settle in by using a hot water bottle, well wrapped in a towel, to keep her warm and cosy on her first night away from her mother and siblings.

You will have plenty of things to prepare for before you bring your new kitten home. You will need to provide one or more litter trays (one for each cat and one on each floor of the house), suitable litter (not too dusty for kittens), and food and water bowls, as well as toys and beds. Shallow bowls are best, especially for kittens, so that they can reach the food and water easily. Ceramic bowls are preferable to plastic, which can leach harmful residues in the long term, while stainless

---

CHECKLIST FOR YOUR KITTEN'S FIRST NIGHT

- Make sure they have a familiar blanket or toy.
- Use a hot water bottle, wrapped in a towel or blanket for warmth.
- Provide the background noise of a ticking clock or a radio at low volume, for comfort.
- Use a few drops of Dr Bach's Rescue Remedy in water or food to help counter any anxiety or shock.

steel can be cold to the tongue. Remember that kittens have very sharp claws and love to explore, so it will pay to remove any treasured items of furniture or priceless velvet curtains before your new feline arrives!

You don't have to spend a fortune on new cat beds: a cardboard box with one side cut down and lined with a soft blanket will do just fine. However, having said that, many cats prefer enclosed, igloo-type beds, so that they feel safe and enclosed, so this may be one type of bed to buy new. Whatever the style, ensure that the bed is easily washable and put it in a quiet place, such as a spare bedroom, ready for your new arrival. The same goes for toys; you can be inventive and make a feather on a string on a rod or use a simple ping-pong ball.

If your kitten will be able to go outside when she is old enough, then it is time to think about what sort of cat-flap you need to install. Either a magnetic collar or your cat's microchip will activate some of the best cat-flaps (*see* Microchipping and Identification section below). This ensures that only your cat will be allowed access, helping to prevent problems of marauding neighbourhood cats coming into your home.

SOCIALIZATION

Socialization is the process by which your kitten learns about the world around her and learns to accept everyday sights, smells, sounds and routines as normal. This allows her to become accustomed to all the potentially scary things that she will come into contact with throughout her life, such as people and noisy household appliances. Socialization is very important for well-adjusted kittens; unfortunately, many of the problem behaviours that later emerge in cats can be traced back to inadequate home environments or poor handling in their crucial early days and weeks.

The key socialization period for kittens is between two and seven weeks of age, and this is when they develop their social manners. In most cases the kitten will already have gone through this stage by the time they go to a new owner, at around eight to twelve weeks of age. Hence the home environment that you choose to get your kitten from can play

Provide your new kitten with a familiar bed or blanket.

a role in the temperament and character of the cat that you end up with. Kittens that come from busy, family homes where they have been exposed to all the usual household sights and sounds (dishwashers, washing machines, vacuum cleaners) are far less likely to be distressed by these things when they are older. Similarly, if your kitten has been used to handling and plenty of human contact from an early age, she is more likely to tolerate or even seek out human contact as an adult.

Familiarity breeds contentment

Exploring new environments and meeting new people can all help to socialize young kittens to life in the home. If, however, your kitten was raised in a cage in an outdoor cattery, or indeed was a stray, she will be more likely to be very timid and anxious about people and many household situations as an adult. This will be due to her poor socialization in her crucial early weeks of life.

Therefore, the aim of every owner who brings up a litter of kittens is to make sure that they are able to take everyday things in their stride. They will need to introduce their charges to lots of sights, sounds and experiences in the home environment and to give them the opportunity to investigate new things with confidence. Exposing kittens to a wide variety of sights, sounds, tastes, textures, smells and experiences (such as barking dogs, young children, trips in the car and the sound and sensation of the cat-flap) will help to produce calmer and more confident adult cats.

Of course, in addition to the environmental factors of their early home life, kittens also learn how to behave by observing their mother and siblings, as well as by instinct. They learn social and hunting skills by playing with their sib-

> ### HANDLING
>
> It is a good idea for kittens to be handled little and often every day whilst they are growing up. Multiple short sessions of just a few minutes each is the best way of doing this and will be least stressful for your kitten. You can use these interactions to help your kitten get used to being touched all over and having her paws, ears and mouth checked (making it easier for the vet later on!).

lings and testing the boundaries of what is allowed at home. In addition, genetic predispositions inherited from their parents will also help to shape and form every kitten's individual responses and personality traits. Indeed, there is often a huge difference in friendliness and overall responses between littermates that can only be explained by a difference in their genetic make-up, since environmental influences were exactly the same for every kitten.

Being handled often and by different people increases a cat's sociability towards

Practise handling your kitten from day one.

humans. In fact research has shown that kittens that are regularly handled by four or five different people before they are seven weeks of age will be more sociable towards people as adult cats, and more likely to initiate social interaction with them.

Of course, socialization and learning doesn't just occur in the period between two and seven weeks of age. It continues throughout your cat's life, so there are still plenty of new experiences for your kitten to get to grips with when she arrives in her new home with you, usually at around eight weeks of age.

FEEDING

Most kittens go to their new homes long after weaning, so you won't have to deal with the weaning process unless you have bred the kittens yourself. Weaning usually begins at around three to four weeks of age, when the queen will start to spend less and less time in the nest suckling her kittens. Initially, the kittens should be offered milk replacer diluted one to one with water in a flat shallow dish, and then gradually introduced to either moistened dry food or tinned food mixed with a little of the milk replacer solution. The kittens' teeth and gums will still be quite sensitive at this stage as they won't be used to eating hard foods, so moistening the food is important.

Kitten food ('growth diet' or 'kitten diet') is especially formulated for growing kittens. Queens would also have been fed this diet throughout their pregnancy in order to meet the extra demands of the gestation period. Cats' food preferences are established early in life. So by offering your kitten a mixture of wet and dry food in a range of different flavours, you will be broadening her adult palate so that she may accept a wider variety of food types as an adult.

Kittens need several small meals throughout the day as they have smaller stomachs and a higher metabolic rate than adults. As they mature kittens can gradually be weaned onto fewer main meals a day to suit your regime (*see* Chapter 7). They will usually need to be on 'kitten/growth' diet until they reach adulthood at around a year old, at which point they can gradually be weaned onto an adult diet.

NO MILK PLEASE!

After weaning most cats are lactose intolerant and can no longer digest milk properly. This means that although cats do love milk, it usually gives them an upset tummy and can cause diarrhoea. If you are keen to offer your cat milk for a treat choose special lactose-free 'cat milk' from the pet shop – but remember that this is high in calories and so is not a healthy choice for obese cats.

PLAYTIME

Kittens learn through a combination of observation, play and experimentation, with their amusing antics and games helping them to develop the mental and physical skills they need as adults. They use play to learn about the world around them, how to interact with people, other cats and objects, and how to form relationships. So providing your kitten with plenty of distractions and interacting with her in games and playtime is a crucial part of her development.

Although in their very early weeks a kitten's behaviour and attention is directed principally towards their mother and siblings, from around eight weeks their attention moves towards play and object-oriented behaviour. This is when their in-built desire to stalk, chase and pounce starts to kick in – a key skill for a predator species.

As they try out their hunting skills, kittens will naturally try to chase and catch almost anything that seems fair game, including your hands and feet. Whilst a few playful nips from a kitten may seem trivial, it is crucial that you never let this behaviour take root because an adult cat who thinks that it is a game to bite at hands and feet will not be popular. Thus you should never use your hands or feet as fun moving targets for her to chase. If your kitten does ever nip you in play, immediately stop what you are doing and turn away. Slowly remove your hands or feet from her and show her that it is not a game. She should then soon learn that using her teeth quickly puts an end to the game, which should be incentive enough to stop this behaviour from continuing.

Toys and games
Keep your kitten busy and happy by pro-

Make time to play with your kitten.

viding her with plenty of safe facilities for climbing, investigating and exploring, and change these around frequently so as to boost her opportunities for exploration, learning and play. Give your kitten lots of light and easily manipulated toys in a variety of different shapes, textures and with various squeaky sounds.

Using interactive toys such as a feather on a string or similar 'fishing-rod' games helps to engage kittens and make for enjoyable playtimes. It is especially important to make time to play with your kitten if she is on her own; one advantage of having siblings is that they can play together and entertain themselves.

The great outdoors
If your kitten will have access to the outdoors, then there will come a time when she is old enough and big enough to be allowed out. This is usually after she (or he) has been neutered (to prevent any risk of unwanted pregnancies), and possibly also microchipped, at around five to six months of age. By this stage most youngsters will literally be climbing the walls in their desire to get out and explore the big wide world! It will undoubtedly be a worrying time for you as you allow your cat outside for the first time.

Once your cat's behaviour indicates that she feels settled and confident enough to venture outside, have a good look at your backyard or garden to ensure that it is safe and cat-friendly. Make sure that there are places for your cat to hide and survey her new territory, as well as easy access to the door and cat-flap in case she wants to run back inside. It is a good idea to supervise your cat's first outing and for it to take place around a mealtime, so that you can easily tempt her back inside if you need to. Doing it at the weekend, and in the morning, gives you plenty of time to supervise your cat as she explores her new area in daylight. Never leave your cat outside unsupervised until you are happy that she is well adjusted to her new environment and knows her way home. It is a good idea to condition your cat to learn to come back into the house when she hears a particular sound, such as the rattling of her food container.

The cat-friendly garden

Making your garden 'feline-friendly' is as important for your cat's mental and emotional well-being as it is for her physical health. Whatever its size, there are simple but effective ways of making your garden as relaxing and rewarding a place for your cat as it is for you. Cats need to be able to hunt, stalk, chase and explore, and a garden is the perfect place for them to be able to express these natural instincts.

To make your garden cat-friendly, give them plenty of places to hide and high-up spots where they can survey their territory; try to think of your garden in 3D. Trees with low, flexible branches, such as Birches, can provide switches and sticks that make fun chase-and-pounce games for cats. They can, of course, also be excellent for climbing, as well as being Nature's very own scratching posts to help keep your cat's claws strong and healthy. Your garden needs to be exciting enough to warrant exploring and playing in, but also, crucially, it needs to be a place where your cat feels safe and secure. Stimulate all your cat's senses with a range of plants of different heights, scents and textures. Make part of your garden into a mini-jungle, so that your cat can stalk and track butterflies and insects. Don't forget to leave a bowl of water outdoors, in case your cat gets thirsty. Also, provide your cat with a secluded, dug-over area that she can use as a toilet and make sure other parts of

SAFETY FIRST

Making sure that your garden doesn't contain any feline hazards is vital. Ideally you would not be using any chemicals in your garden. However, if you do use fertilizers and insecticides, make sure that they are not toxic for your cat and that any bottles and packaging are tightly sealed and stored safely in the garden shed. There is a long list of common garden plants, including flowers such as lilies, daffodils and chrysanthemums, as well as certain shrubs and trees, that can be poisonous to cats. This is because, as a species, cats have a less efficient detoxification system in their bodies so are susceptible to certain plant compounds (such as salicylates) that do not affect other animals. Thankfully, however, cats do not generally attempt to consume these flowers when they are in the garden. Most problems occur with houseplants, so extra care must be taken here not to have any known poisonous flowers (such as lilies) in the house. If you are in any doubt about the plants in your garden and the safety of your cat, have a word with your vet.

the flowerbed (that you don't want her to use) have close groundcover plants and little bare soil. If your cat tends to be intimidated by neighbourhood cats then make your garden as difficult for them to get into as possible.

TRAINING

Kittenhood is the perfect time to begin to lay down any house rules that you may want to instil in your cat, such as not jumping up onto kitchen work surfaces and not scratching the sofa. It will take time and patience, as well as an understanding of how a cat's mind works, but they *can* be trained and will respond well to rewards.

The best way to begin any training session is to choose a small, quiet room where there are few distractions and time it for just before your kitten is due to be fed. Keep the sessions short and sweet, just a few minutes at once, and always reward with a food treat or a game (most kittens are motivated by food rewards).

Training will basically be a combination of positive rewards (yummy treats) offered immediately after your kitten or

LITTER TRAINING

Kittens learn from their mother and will copy her. They can start to be shown how to use a litter tray from as early as three weeks of age. It is safest to use woodchip-type litter to start with as some kittens try to eat it! You can help by standing your kitten in the litter tray and helping them to pass motions (*see* box 'Helping kittens to pass motions'). Litter trays must be easily accessible, with shallow sides, because young kittens, although naturally clean, don't yet have great control.

Litter training.

cat has done the right thing, and using negative association with anything that you don't want her to do. For example, you can use double-sided sticky tape on your kitchen worktop, so that if your cat jumps up onto it she gets an unpleasant feeling on her feet and so is disinclined to do it again. Similarly, a cat that's just about to scratch the arm of your leather sofa gets a shot of water fired near her (but not at her) from a water pistol. The aim of this kind of training is to get your kitten or cat to associate a negative feeling, such as a shock distraction (*never* pain), with certain actions. That way you are encouraging her to naturally avoid doing the things that you don't want her to do. An unexpected spritz of water or a sharp hissing noise from you can quickly discourage unwanted behaviour in your cat as it will feel unpleasant as well as being a sudden distraction from what she is doing. If you are dissuading your kitten from scratching the sofa arm then ensure that you provide her with a proper scratching post nearby, so that she can readily use this instead. Likewise, remember that part of the reason that your kitten may have wanted to go up onto the kitchen worktop was because she likes to be up in high places to survey her domain and stay out of the way. So provide your kitten with several high-up resting places where she is allowed to go instead.

Using rewards can be done, for example, if you are getting your kitten or youngster used to using the cat-flap. Every time she hops through it offer her a treat. Similarly, if you want your cat to be trained to come when you call her (handy for when you need to take her to the vets, for instance), offer her a treat when she comes running. To help her get used to going in the cat carrier make sure that you leave it somewhere accessible, with food rewards inside. That way your kitten will learn to associate going inside it with a treat.

INHERITED CONDITIONS

Pedigree cats can be more likely than domestic moggies to suffer from genetic disorders, simply because they come from a smaller gene pool. Each particular breed may have a susceptibility to certain inherited diseases or conditions, so always look

Kittens can be susceptible to illness.

into any potential problems in your chosen breed before you purchase a kitten. For example, an inherited heart condition (hypertrophic cardiomyopathy) has been identified in the Maine Coon and Ragdoll breeds due to certain genetic defects. It has also been found that an inherited kidney disease (Autosomal dominant polycystic kidney disease, or AD-PKD) is more common in Persian cats and Exotic Shorthairs and other related breeds. Conscientious and reputable breeders will be well aware of the potential problems in their chosen breed and will carry out the necessary screening tests for them. In the case of the heart condition in the Maine Coon and Ragdolls, there are certain gene tests and ultrasound scans that are used to help identify susceptible individuals. There is also a gene test available for AD-PKD.

Added to this, your vet will examine your new kitten carefully on her first visit, as some inherited conditions may be picked up on at an early stage. This is part of the routine check-over from nose to tail, listening to her heart, looking in her eyes, and feeling your kitten all over, so that any problems are picked up as soon as possible.

MICROCHIPPING AND IDENTIFICATION

At around the time of her first veterinary check-up and first vaccination you may choose to have your kitten microchipped. A microchip is an electronic chip about the size of a grain of rice that is inserted, by injection, just under the skin between the shoulder blades. It consists of a unique number that links to a computer database containing your contact details and basic information about your cat. If she gets lost and ends up at a vet's

Pedigree cats come from a smaller gene pool than moggies.

or rescue centre, then by scanning the chip they will find your contact details and you stand the best chance of being reunited. Don't forget to change your contact details if you move house. Microchips are a mandatory part of the process for taking your cat abroad under the Pet Passport scheme.

You may also want to consider an additional means of identifying your cat, such as a collar with an identification disc. Make sure you choose a collar with a quick-release mechanism in case your cat gets caught up in it. Some owners who want to discourage their cats from catching birds put a bell on the collar.

KITTEN HEALTH AND COMMON AILMENTS

Kittens face many stresses on their immune system and this can make them more susceptible to illness. First, they are under more stress due to leaving their mum and siblings, and then there is the change in digestive processes associated with weaning and often a change of

diet when they reach their new home. Added to this, they are also getting used to a new home and new people and have many new things to learn. All of these factors can make your kitten more susceptible to disease. The list below is a brief guide to some of the most common ailments that kittens can suffer from, alongside tips for safe home treatment. (A more comprehensive list of conditions affecting adult cats and kittens, can be found in Chapter 9.)

Always remember that if you have any doubts about your kitten's health or welfare then you should have them checked over straight away by your vet.

Diarrhoea
This is commonly due to the fact that a kitten's digestive system has to both adapt to solid food and get used to a new diet. Either worms or a bacterial or viral infection may also cause diarrhoea in kittens.

In mild cases
If your kitten remains bright and otherwise well and has a good appetite, then

offer her bland food, such as chicken and rice, little and often, allowing her digestive system the chance to rest and repair. Give her about a tablespoon of food six to eight times a day. Continue this diet for a few days and then gradually reintroduce your kitten's usual food, if all is going well.

Using probiotics is another way of supporting your kitten's digestive system and helping to resolve mild diarrhoea. These usually come in the form of capsules, which can be added to your kitten's food and will help to repopulate her digestive system with 'good bugs'. Some people give their kittens a probiotic (such as lactobacilli) supplement as a matter of course, to help prevent diarrhoea and other gastrointestinal upsets, when they arrive at their new home. Vets often prescribe proprietary pastes or powders that contain both probiotics and kaolin, in the treatment of diarrhoea. The probiotics help to re-establish the intestinal bugs, while kaolin is a clay-like mineral that helps make formed stools again.

In more severe cases
Taking your kitten to the vet is important if the diarrhoea has blood in it, if her tummy seems painful or is bloated, if she is vomiting, or if she seems lethargic and is off her food. Your vet will be able to check your kitten all over, and make sure that she doesn't have a temperature, that she isn't dehydrated and that she doesn't have any sign of a blockage or other problem in her tummy. If your vet has any concerns they may admit your kitten for treatment. Taking in a sample of your kitten's diarrhoea, in a plastic bag or jar, can often be helpful for the vet, who will send it to a laboratory for analysis. This will confirm if the diarrhoea is due to bacte-

ria or a parasite (an intestinal worm, such as roundworm), or other common kitten diarrhoea bugs. It is important to get this diagnostic test done if the diarrhoea is in any way ongoing, because it may require specific veterinary medication, such as wormers or antibiotics, to clear it up. It is also important because some of these diseases are zoonotic, which means they can be passed on to people.

Cat flu
Cat flu or upper respiratory tract disease, is usually caused by the feline herpesvirus (FHV-1) and feline calicivirus (FCV). Infection can cause signs ranging from mild to very severe, including sore throat, mouth ulcers, coughing, sneezing, nasal discharge, conjunctivitis and even pneumonia. Some cats recover fully in a few days, whilst others take much longer and can even suffer permanent damage to the eyes and nose. All kittens should be vaccinated against these viruses as this helps to protect them from severe illness. Vaccination, however, does not prevent all cases of infection and kittens especially can be affected, as their immune systems are not as robust as an adult's. These viruses are highly infectious and can be carried by cats that show no signs of illness themselves but can still pass them on to others.

If your kitten shows any signs of cat flu you should take her to the vet straight away to have her checked over and for suitable treatment to be prescribed. You can help to keep her eyes and nose clear of discharge by gently wiping them with damp cotton wool.

Fleas
A heavy flea burden can be a serious complaint for kittens because a large volume of fleas can cause anaemia. If

your kitten is affected you will be able to clearly see the fleas as they are visible to the naked eye, and will jump off your kitten and onto you! It is important to have your kitten checked over by the vet if you suspect fleas, as they will be able to weigh your kitten and provide the correct treatment. Because the cat flea can carry the larval stage of the tapeworm (*Dipylidium caninum*), worming is an important part of treatment. (*See also* Chapter 8.)

Ear mites

These are spider-like parasites, just visible to the naked eye as tiny white specks, that live right down inside the ear canals and can commonly affect kittens and young cats. The mites (*Otodectes cynotis*) feed on the debris and ear wax in the ear canal and can cause a lot of irritation and discomfort for kittens. Cats and kittens with ear mites will scratch their ears and shake their heads because of the itchiness, and a lot of brown, waxy debris will be produced in the ear. Your vet will usually be able to identify the mites by having a good look down your kitten's ear canal using a special instrument called an otoscope, and by taking a sample of the waxy discharge. Your kitten may need some conventional anti-parasitic medications to eradicate ear mites, as the herbal solution outlined in Chapter 8 may not be enough on its own. Any medicated drops should be used exactly according to the directions from the vet, as mites go through lifecycles, and the adults need to be killed as they emerge over three weeks. Ear mites are highly contagious to other kittens, cats and also to dogs.

Accidents and injuries

Unfortunately, kittens have a tendency to be in the wrong place at the wrong time and they can end up being tripped over or even stepped on, or dropped from your hands. In any such situation it is crucial to take your kitten to the vet to be thoroughly checked over to make sure that no internal damage has been done and that nothing is broken. In addition, the homeopathic remedy for shock, aconite, can be given as soon as possible after the incident, giving a single dose of a 30c. In addition, arnica, the homeopathic remedy for trauma and bruising, can also be used. The dose of arnica will usually be 30c twice daily for a few days, depending on the extent of any injury. Your kitten may also need a few doses of Dr Bach's Rescue Remedy, to help her to recover from the shock. None of these complementary remedies should affect the treatments that your vet may need to give your kitten, so they are usually suitable to be given in the car on the way to the vet.

Reaction to vaccination

Mild reactions, such as transient pain at the injection site or being slightly quiet for twenty-four hours, are not unusual after a kitten's first vaccination. However, if these symptoms go on for longer than this period, or seem in any way more serious, then it is time for a checkup by the vet to make sure your kitten does not have a temperature or any other problem. The homeopathic remedy that is often given to animals that seem a little unwell after a vaccination, or indeed have any kind of reaction to it, is thuja. This can be given at a 30c potency up to twice a day usually for two or three days after the vaccine. Some people use it routinely after vaccination, whether there are any adverse effects in their animal or not.

5 THE ELDERLY CAT

Advances in nutrition and health care mean that many cats are enjoying a much longer lifespan than they used to, living well into their late teens and even early twenties. The first signs of ageing can start anywhere between seven and eleven years of age, with most cats entering their 'senior years' from around ten onwards. In this chapter we will examine the most common signs of ageing and what you can do to make life for your senior cat as comfortable and rewarding as possible. It will become clear that by simply making a few small changes to her everyday care, you can make a great difference to your elderly cat's comfort and health. Knowing what to expect as your cat grows older gives you the best possible chance of being able to offer her a long and rewarding retirement. We will also discover how natural holistic therapies are especially suited to the elderly cat.

THE AGEING PROCESS

For the majority of cats, the ageing process will be gradual and graceful and they will go on to live full, happy and rewarding lives as senior citizens. It is down to the combined effects of genetic make-up, individuality and circumstances that tend to determine how your cat copes with growing older.

As your cat ages you are likely to notice a slowing down, as she suffers with stiffness and arthritis and spends more time curled up in her favourite chair. Although ageing is, of course, a normal process rather than a disease, it does nonetheless lead to a gradual and inevitable decline in the functioning capacity of many of the body's systems, including the heart, liver and kidneys, to name just a few.

You may also notice changes in her routine, as your cat is no longer able to roam as far as she used to or to get up onto favourite, high resting places. Added to this, your senior feline may also show

Some cats live into their twenties.

some age-related signs of a change in personality or temperament. Changes in drinking habits are a potential cause for concern because if your older cat begins to either drink more at each sitting or to make more frequent visits to the water bowl, this can be a sign of kidney disease or even diabetes.

Whether it is a physical or a mental change, it is always wise to act on any significant alteration in your cat's daily habits, because the signs of ageing and those of certain medical conditions are indistinguishable to the untrained eye. Thus regular medical checks for your senior companion are important, so that any problems can be picked up and treated at an early stage.

There are certainly ways to help any senior cat cope with the changes associated with ageing and enable your old friend to live more comfortably in her retirement years.

CARING FOR YOUR ELDERLY CAT

This requires you to look at the world from your ageing cat's point of view. Think about how she usually gets around and how this may become compromised as she becomes less energetic and less mobile. How are you able to change her everyday environment at home so that your cat can still reach her favourite snooze-spots and easily access her bowls and litter trays, for example? The good news is that by simply making a few small adjustments to your home, and to how you care for your ageing companion, you can make sure that your cat is still able to enjoy a good quality of life as she grows older.

Routine and familiarity
Senior cats are fond of their routine and like a peaceful life. Avoid any unnecessary changes and ensure that everything she needs – beds, bowls, litter trays, and so on – are easily accessible and that your cat's daily life is as predictable as possible. Now that she is older, your cat may have a much smaller territory and may

Cats sleep more in old age.

TOP TIPS FOR ELDERLY CAT CARE

- Arrange for regular vet check-ups.
- Provide your cat with at least two indoor litter trays that she can access easily.
- Cover slippery floors with non-slip mats.
- Feed her smaller but more frequent meals.
- Keep her claws trimmed (especially the dew claws).
- Provide her with at least two beds in comfortable, quiet places and use insulating fleece for bedding.
- Play with her for a few minutes every day to keep her mind and body alert.
- Stick to a regular daily routine and keep any changes to a minimum.
- On warm, sunny days take your cat outside to sit on your lap and sunbathe.
- If you are away on holiday, arrange for someone to come in and feed your cat at home so she can stay in familiar surroundings.
- Give her a daily massage and groom her.

Senior cats enjoy a quiet life.

prefer to stay around the house much more than she used to. This makes it especially important that this reduced 'home domain' provides her with all the comfort and stimulation she needs. It may also be helpful to lay coverings on slippery or wooden floors so that your cat doesn't slip as she gets around, as senior joints can be weaker and more prone to injury. With your help, even the most frail and elderly cat can still enjoy a good quality of life.

Comfort and warmth
Older cats are more sensitive to the cold, and benefit from a soft, warm bed away from draughts. For those that really do suffer from the cold, the use of heated pads or good old-fashioned woolly blankets is a necessary addition, especially in the winter. If you are using a heated pad make sure that you never leave it turned on overnight or when you are out. Also ensure that your cat can quickly move away from it if she needs to, for instance if she gets too hot.

A routine check-up for an older cat.

over, checking for any worrying lumps or bumps and assessing the range of movement of her joints. They will also listen to your cat's heart and lungs, to make sure that her cardiovascular system is still working well. Your cat will also be weighed, because weight loss can be an indicator of underlying disease, as can any significant alterations in her drinking habits or appetite. Your vet will usually offer a 'geriatric cat' blood test, and may also run a urine screen, to help them assess how your cat's internal organs are working.

Grooming and nail care

Cats are often less able to groom themselves or to keep their nails in good condition as they grow older. This is almost always because they find it uncomfortable or even painful to groom themselves and they are not conditioning their claws by using scratching posts, as they used

Regular vet checks

Senior cats usually benefit from more regular MOTs than younger cats. This ensures that you can pick up any medical condition as early as possible, so that any necessary treatment will be more effective. Your vet will be best placed to advise you on how often your cat should be seen (this may depend on whether she is on any ongoing medications), but it is usually every six to twelve months.

These senior health assessments are important because the normal signs of old age, such as slowing down, lethargy, fussy appetite and stiffness, need to be differentiated from the early signs of a disease condition. Your vet will be able to manipulate and palpate your cat all

---

CLAW CLIPPING

If your cat is amenable and has had her nails clipped from a young age, then you shouldn't have much trouble doing it for her more often in old age. Sit comfortably with your cat on a table in front of you and, holding each of her paws in turn, gently press behind each claw to extend it. Then, positioning the clippers at right angles to the claw, cut the tip to remove the sharp tip (you may need an assistant to hold your cat still). Always ensure that you clip well in front of the visible pink 'quick' of each claw, as this is the sensitive part that will bleed. If you are in any doubt, or you have a wriggly cat, it is far better to get your vet to do it, or at least give you a demonstration first.

Senior cats need regular grooming.

to. It may be sore for them to stretch and groom all parts of their bodies. A lack of grooming can also be a sign of dental pain (toothache). Overlong nails can be a serious problem because as a cat's nails are curved they can actually grow into the footpads, which is very painful. Elderly cats should have their nails checked every eight weeks or so; if you are unable to cut them yourself, you will need to take her to the vet for this.

Helping senior cats to groom themselves is an important aspect of their

Older cats need warmer, more supportive beds.

daily care, to maintain their coat in good condition so that it is properly warm and waterproof. It also helps to improve their well-being, as cats generally hate to be unkempt. Don't forget that arthritic or thin cats may find it uncomfortable to be groomed with a regular brush, so choose a soft, baby brush instead. Finally, assist your senior cat's daily ablutions by regularly wiping away any discharge from her eyes and nose.

Beds and bedding
The sort of bed your ageing cat sleeps on is important. As she gets older, your cat will appreciate a warmer and more supportive bed. Older pets generally have thinner skin and feel the cold more than younger ones; added to this, arthritic joints will benefit from firmer beds with more padding to protect them. You can buy orthopaedic beds that have a memory foam mattress and these are especially beneficial for older cats. Also, consider how easy it is for your cat to get into and out of her bed, and whether she can reach it without bother. Ensuring that the sides are not too high, that it is not in a position that makes it awkward for her to get into it and that it is not in a draught are all helpful considerations. Make sure that your senior cat has a range of different resting places, to watch the world go by or to get some peace and quiet. A quiet retreat is important because elderly cats can be less tolerant when disturbed from sleep than they used to be. You can help your senior cat to reach her favoured bed by placing cushions or books as stepping-stones onto chairs, windowsills and sofas, or you can even buy special cat steps or stairs!

Litter trays
Even if your cat has always used the gar-

den for her toilet, as she grows older she may be unwilling or unable to get outside as much as she used to. This can either be because of painful arthritic joints making steps or cat-flaps tricky to navigate or because she no longer wants to go out into the wet and cold or to have to confront neighbourhood cats. It is also true that bladder and bowel control can deteriorate with age. Having a few litter trays in the house and making access to the garden easier will be important ways of helping your senior cat to maintain her house training. Choose litter trays that have low sides and are easy for your cat to get to without having to jump or climb or go past a busy part of the house – remember, your elderly cat prefers the quiet life.

Deteriorating senses

Cats with deteriorating eyesight or hearing need extra care and attention. They may be startled more easily when you approach them, may fail to respond to your calls, or may be more accident prone around the house. Try to be patient and make allowances. Always approach your elderly cat slowly, so that she knows you are there before you touch her, and try to keep the layout and furniture at home as familiar as possible.

Eyesight

As well as being a normal sign of ageing, deteriorating senses, especially eyesight, can be a symptom of disease, which unless treated properly can lead to total blindness. This is why it is important to have your senior cat checked over by a vet as soon as you notice any deterioration in her eyesight, so that any appropriate treatment can be started straight away.

Hearing loss

Diminished hearing can cause some cats

to become more anxious and demanding, with night-time yowling and wandering. However, this can also be a sign of senility (*see* box), and is quite common in senior cats. The best thing to do if your cat does become demanding and restless at night (after having her checked over by the vet) is to make sure that she is settled in a warm and comfortable bed and then do not respond to her yowling. This is because once you start responding to her cry, your cat will usually continue to do it, as she knows she'll attract your attention this way. It is far better to ensure that she is warm and comfortable and try to settle her by using a few drops of Dr Bach's Rescue Remedy in her supper, or by using a pheromone diffuser to help her to relax.

Behavioural changes

As your cat gets older you may notice changes in her personality and demeanour. This can be linked to physical ailments (related to pain, for instance, or to hyperthyroidism), or to mental issues (such as senility). It may be that your cat is more needy and clingy than she used to be, becoming more vocal and following you around the house wanting attention. Some older cats, having been stand-offish their whole lives, become more affectionate as they get older. In contrast, others turn inwards and become more antisocial as they grow older, preferring to be on their own and to sleep a lot more.

Confusion and disorientation can also be a problem in senior cats (like senility or dementia in people), linked to ageing of the brain. In these cases you can help to orientate your cat by having different scents, sounds and textures associated with different areas of the house. For example, you can add a few drops of lavender oil on a blanket in a particular bed, to help your cat remember where she is.

Senile dementia

It has recently been realised that cats, like people, can develop a form of senile dementia. The symptoms of dementia in cats can range from mild confusion to severe anxiety. Taken on their own, the signs of senility can be subtle, but when combined they are significant and can really affect your cat's quality of life. The medical term for senility is 'cognitive dysfunction'. It is a gradual process linked to a combination of reduced blood flow to the brain and chronic free radical damage (*see* box below). Early research indicates that this disease in cats has similarities to age-related conditions in dogs (canine cognitive dysfunction), as well as in humans, where it is comparable to senile dementia and Alzheimer's.

At present there is no specific treatment for feline dementia, but a range of supportive treatments is available that can help to delay the condition's progress and even reverse some of the symptoms. Some of the more commonly suggested

---

THE POWER OF ANTIOXIDANTS

As they get older all the cells in a cat's body, but especially in the brain, become less efficient at defending themselves from the ongoing attack of molecules called 'free radicals'. Although potentially damaging, free radicals do not usually cause problems because they are removed by the body's antioxidant system. However, in old age the body needs extra support to combat the potential damage caused by free radicals, and hence benefits from the addition of antioxidants in the diet or via supplements. Beneficial antioxidants include vitamins A, C and E and the minerals selenium and zinc.

---

supportive treatments include a diet that is rich in antioxidants, and medications that help enhance blood flow to the brain or have a protective effect on the nervous system tissue.

In humans, however, there is one particular plant that has traditionally been used in the treatment of senility and symptoms of brain ageing. *Ginkgo biloba*

FELINE DEMENTIA

Cats, like people, can suffer from a form of dementia as they grow older. Signs that your cat may be suffering from this include confusion and disorientation in familiar places; sleep disturbances, excessive vocalization and restlessness at night; house-soiling; and a change in activity and appetite levels. There may also be changes in social interactions, where cats become either very withdrawn or overly demanding. Always have your cat checked by your vet if you are concerned that she is showing any of these symptoms.

Ginkgo biloba *is a key herbal remedy for brain ageing.*

is one of the oldest plant medicines on earth. It improves blood flow, and hence oxygenation, to the brain, and also enhances nervous system function. In the future this amazing herb may have a role in the treatment of cats with dementia.

One-to-one time

Whatever the cause of your ageing cat's mental or physical problems, make sure that you offer them quality time for attention and fussing, as well as play, every day. Build an appropriate level of physical and mental exercise into your elderly cat's daily routine to help keep her engaged and active. This can be as simple as introducing (or reintroducing) games such as a feather on a string, but allowing your cat to play gently whilst she is lying on a cushion or in her bed. Try to develop a daily routine for engaging your senior cat in a sociable activity like this, so that the mental stimulation of the game becomes a learned behaviour. This may even help to ward off senility, as it keeps your cat's brain active. You can use puzzle feeders and toys that enable her to feel engaged and stimulated for short periods, even if it's just moving from one comfortable bed to another.

You can also stimulate an interest in hunting for food by placing bits of your cat's favourite food around the house, semi-hidden, for her to search out. Finally, make life rewarding for your elderly cat by spending time gently massaging or stroking her. This can help her to feel calm and relaxed as well as allowing you to notice any areas of discomfort, or to detect any lumps and bumps.

Reduced mobility and arthritis

These problems deserve a particular mention because they are such common symptoms of ageing. There is no getting away

Keep your elderly cat mentally and physically active.

from the fact that mobility declines as cats get older, and senior cats can become quite stiff and sore in their joints. However, regular activity is still important in order to maintain muscle mass and flexibility. So encouraging your cat to move around the house every day, however old and frail she is, can be advantageous for maintaining longer-term strength and mobility.

It can be quite difficult to spot pain and arthritis in cats because they are not often overtly lame, as dogs can be. Instead, cats that have painful joints will tend to sleep more; they may be reluctant to climb up onto usual or favourite resting places and perhaps become resentful of handling or grooming. You may therefore notice a change in their daily habits, as well as an increase in the time spent sleeping. Pay attention to any alterations in your cat's activity patterns, or problems with stiffness and jumping up.

Arthritis is a term used to describe inflammation of joints, from the Greek *arthro* ('joint') and itis ('inflammation'). It causes pain and a reduced range of movement. The arthritis of the senior cat is also known as 'osteoarthritis' or 'degenerative joint disease', and is a common age-related condition. Their joints become stiff and painful after a lifetime's wear and tear, and because of the degeneration of the protective cartilage cushioning of the joint surface.

When it comes to arthritis, prevention is much better than cure. The mainstay of conventional treatment is symptomatic pain relief, and slowing the progression of the joint degeneration. Holistic therapies and the use of joint supplements aim to address the underlying joint degeneration and systemic imbalance, as well as easing the pain. Keeping your cat's weight down as she gets older will be another helpful way of reducing any extra load on painful joints and will hence keep your cat more mobile and comfortable.

Treatment options
Pain undermines quality of life and mood, which means that how your cat feels physically will affect her emotional equilibrium. With a range of possibilities when it comes to pain relief and treatment, your cat should not have to suffer discomfort.

Conventional medications
If your cat is suffering pain with her arthritic joints and showing signs of discomfort, then your vet may well put her onto an anti-inflammatory medication to relieve the symptoms. By reducing the inflammation around the problematic joints, your cat should be able to move around without pain, and hence maintain strength and general fitness as well as quality of life.

Various types of anti-inflammatory drug are used for arthritis, but the most common are the non-steroidal anti-inflammatories (NSAIDS). These are usually tablets or liquids given daily over the long-term, or they may just be required as a few doses to manage a 'flare-up'. Although they are highly effective as painkillers, possible side effects and the fact that they are simply alleviating the symptoms are the limiting factors for using NSAIDS as the sole way of managing arthritis in an elderly cat. With the wide range of complementary medicines and therapies on offer, your cat should be able to benefit from an integrated approach to treatment.

Homeopathy
A handful of homeopathic remedies are indicated for use in arthritis. Because homeopathy works by matching your cat's individual symptoms to the particular action of the remedy, selecting the right one will depend on your careful observation as well as knowledge of the remedies. (*See* Chapter 1.)

Rhus tox is one of the most commonly prescribed remedies for arthritis. This is for cats who are stiff when they first get up after a long rest, but ease up after walking around, and those who are much affected by the damp.

Rhus tox, ruta and arnica (RRA) is often used as a combination remedy. Arnica and ruta are also both useful for treating muscle and ligament strains and sprains.

Bryonia is used for symptoms of arthritis that are much better for resting and worse for warmth – the opposite to rhus tox. When this remedy is indicated, you may notice your cat lies on the affected side in order to keep the painful part of her body as still as possible.

Acupuncture

It will come as no surprise to learn that this, although a highly valuable and effective form of pain relief, is not usually well tolerated by cats! However, if your cat is amenable to it, acupuncture is a very beneficial complementary treatment for aches, pains and stiffness, and is widely used to treat arthritic animals. Because it is a holistic therapy, acupuncture is more than just a form of pain relief; it can enhance your cat's overall well-being by boosting appetite, regulating sleep patterns and supporting liver and kidney function. Acupuncture also stimulates the immune system – another advantage of this form of treatment for the geriatric cat.

Herbal medicine

There are several herbs that have a long history of use for the treatment of arthritis. Ask your vet about the following:

Turmeric: this Indian herb has the active constituent curcumin, well documented as having anti-inflammatory and antioxidant properties.

Boswellia: this herb is well known as a natural anti-inflammatory and is now being included in some of the proprietary mobility products, along with glucosamines and chondroitin.

Devil's Claw: this is a traditional South African herb used for arthritis, as well as for digestive complaints.

Massage and Chiropractic treatment

It is a natural reaction to want to give your cat a gentle stroke or rub when she appears to be in pain or stiff. There really isn't anything fancy or special about mas-

Acupuncture treatment for arthritis.

sage; it is as easy or as complex as you want to make it. You can simply follow your instincts and let your hands and fingers guide you to work on her sore areas, or you can learn some of the healing manipulative techniques such as therapeutic massage or TTouch. The Tellington Touch, or TTouch, is a way of healing your cat using gentle and directed finger touches anywhere on her body (*see* Chapter 1). Your cat can benefit from TTouch to help with a great range of musculoskeletal problems such as arthritis and to enhance health and recovery. Because it is so simple and intuitive, TTouch is a popular method of hands-on treatment for cats.

The simplest approach is a gentle but firm massage all over, but especially along your cat's spine, from head to tail and along each limb down to her feet. This will help to get her circulation going and will be a lovely treat for your older cat to enjoy every day. Of course, if she does not want to be touched, or if you find any sore or painful areas, then she should be checked over at the vets.

Chiropractic adjustment is a physical manipulation technique that helps to realign the spine and can be a highly beneficial treatment for cats suffering from arthritis. (*See* Chapter 1.)

Supplements for arthritis

With the ever-growing array of supplements for the arthritic cat, it becomes increasingly important to understand how they work and what they contain, so that you can choose the best one for your senior citizen. The most commonly used supplements for treating joint pain and arthritis include glucosamine, chondroitin and green-lipped mussel (*see* Chapter 8).

A very elderly cat suffering from hyperthyroidism.

THE SENIOR CAT'S DIET

For all senior cats excess weight gain needs to be avoided at all costs as it puts more stress on their joints (which may be arthritic), as well as extra strain on their heart. Weight loss, on the other hand, may be linked to loss of appetite due to deterioration in a cat's sense of taste and smell as she gets older, or, more commonly, it may be linked to an underlying medical complaint. That's why, with weight loss in particular, a veterinary check-up for your senior cat is a good idea.

Equally, you should appreciate that as she slows down and becomes less active, your cat will usually need fewer calories in her daily rations. However, it is not as simple as just feeding her less: your elderly cat actually needs a different, more nutrient-dense food. Whilst her body is less efficient at extracting all the essential goodness from her food, your cat's ageing body also has a greater requirement for it. Her need for highly digestible essential nutrients has gone up to meet the demands of a lifetime's wear and tear, to counter ongoing degenerative processes and to support her weakened immune system.

The purrfect menu

A senior cat's diet should reflect these specific needs by containing high-quality ingredients that are easily digestible and rich in nutrients and vitamins. This diet should consequently contain fewer toxins, putting less strain on the liver and kidneys, easing the ageing body's workload (in short, choose organic or natural diets). Because the senior diet is more energy and nutrient dense, it can be fed in smaller quantities, to match the reduced appetite of the older cat. Your cat's digestive system will also be more sensitive as she gets older, making it particularly important not to make any abrupt changes to her diet, or to offer her anything new, for risk of tummy upsets. This more delicate digestive tract is also the reason why senior cats are fed a more easily digestible diet (there are many foods formulated for 'senior cats'). The more additives and complex, unnatural ingredients in the food, the greater will be the workload on your cat's digestive system.

Enzymes in the digestive juices help to break down the foodstuffs into the building blocks that the body can use. Probiotics – friendly bacteria – in your cat's intestinal system also play a vital role in digestion, and provide essential vitamins for the body. Therefore by adding an enzyme or probiotic supplement to her diet you can help boost your cat's digestive system, helping her to get the most out of her food (*see* Chapter 7).

Finally, the senior cat's diet needs to be rich in antioxidants. These are present in all healthy, fresh, natural foodstuffs, but can also be given as supplements in their own right. Antioxidants help combat the everyday signs of ageing, so are a particularly important addition to the elderly cat's diet. Most good-quality nutritional supplements contain a base of enzymes and probiotics, as well as multivitamins and antioxidants.

Whilst some cats tend to put on weight as they get older and less active, others have the opposite problem and become very thin as they age. This means that you need to be aware of your senior cat's weight and appetite, and tailor your care and her diet to her individual needs. What is common to all senior cats' diets, though, is the need for them to contain higher levels of antioxidants and vitamins that help to protect their ageing bodies from the damaging effects of free radicals.

Because all cats age in their own way, with different parts of their bodies needing support at various times, you may every so often have to alter their diet to meet these changing needs. Therefore evaluating your cat's individual health status by regular vet checks and blood tests will alert you to any organ systems that need particular support as early as possible.

Chronic kidney failure

If your senior cat is drinking a lot more than normal, then this may be a sign of

DIETARY SUPPORT FOR CHRONIC KIDNEY FAILURE

For cats diagnosed with chronic kidney failure a special restricted protein and phosphorus diet is usually indicated. This is because many of the toxic products that accumulate in the blood in animals with kidney failure are the products of protein breakdown. However, too little protein in the diet can lead to excessive weight loss, so especially formulated commercial 'kidney' or 'renal' diets are usually the best option, where the protein level has been scientifically calculated to be optimum. In addition, these special diets are also low in phosphate, which helps to protect the kidneys from further damage. Prescription renal diets have usually been specially formulated by vets and are sold at veterinary practices.

In traditional Chinese medicine acupuncture is also used to treat kidney disease.

disease (such as kidney disease), so you should have her checked by the vet as soon as possible. There are special prescription diets for age-related conditions such as kidney disease; your vet will be able to advise you on the best diet for your cat if she has been diagnosed with any such complaint.

Chronic kidney failure happens when the kidneys gradually lose their ability to filter and remove waste products from the blood. It is only when between two-thirds and three-quarters of the kidney tissue has been affected that visible signs of kidney failure become apparent. It is diagnosed in around one in five cats over the age of fifteen, but in most elderly cats the cause is unknown.

If, despite your best efforts, your cat refuses to eat the special 'renal' diets and finds them unpalatable, try warming them and mixing them with their regular food. If they still won't touch them, then they will need to have their normal food, but this can contain an added phosphate 'binder' that your vet will prescribe in order to reduce the amount of absorbed phosphate. The bottom line is that a cat with chronic renal failure may well have a poor appetite, so if they don't take to their 'renal' diet then just make sure that you tempt them with something else, as eating regular food is much better than eating nothing!

Dehydration

Although cats of any age can suffer from dehydration, senior cats in particular can be at risk. This is due to a number of different factors, such as reduced mobility (so that they find it more difficult to access their water bowls), confusion or dementia, or as a result of kidney disease or another medical condition. The risk of dehydration obviously increases in hot weather or if your cat is fed exclusively dry food.

The best way of ensuring that your elderly cat does not become dehydrated is to provide access to water in several locations that she can reach easily. Use wide bowls (cats don't like to have their whiskers touching the sides) filled to the brim. Experiment with different types of water container, offering wide, deep bowls in a variety of designs. It is known that cats prefer bowls that are filled to the brim because they like the surface tension that is created.

Once you are familiar with the amount of water that your cat normally drinks on a daily basis, you will be able to spot any changes in her thirst patterns and hence pick up any potential problems early on.

SAYING GOODBYE

As your companion enters the last phase of her life, it can be an agonising time because it is your responsibility to decide when the time is right to say goodbye. Euthanasia is usually the most humane course of action where the prognosis is hopeless or where the continued life of your cat would be painful or undignified for her.

Although there are no hard and fast rules, it is generally always a question of 'quality of life', weighing up the amount of pleasure your cat still gets out of life with the degree that she struggles with physical or mental deterioration. It is often hard to appreciate the overall trend of her quality of life when you are with your cat every day, but it can help to keep a daily record. Thus if her condition seems to vary from one day to the next, as it often does in elderly pets, keeping a daily note of whether she has had a good day or a bad day helps you to see the bigger picture over a few weeks. It is also important to talk it over with your vet, so that you can be sure in your own mind as to exactly what your cat's problems are and the likely prognosis. You can also discuss the options for when it comes to having your senior cat put to sleep (whether it can be done at home or at the surgery).

Euthanasia

When the day comes, you can either take your cat to the surgery or have her euthanased at home. By making the arrangements in advance you will be left with the peace of mind of knowing that your cat enjoyed a fulfilled life where she had love and respect right up until the last moment. In most cases, where possible, it is obviously a more pleasant experience for you as well as your cat to arrange for the vet to do a home visit. This way your cat will be less anxious, will not have to travel in the car and can stay in familiar surroundings.

Euthanasia itself is usually from a lethal injection given into the front leg. The vet will normally have to clip a little of the fur from your cat's leg and is likely to have a nurse helping to hold her. Staying with her whilst she is put to sleep will usually be a great comfort and reassurance for your cat. It will also help if you speak to her, and stroke her. Hearing your voice and feeling your touch will allow her to pass away peacefully, feeling loved and cared for.

SENIOR CAT CARE AND COMMON AILMENTS

Many ailments of the senior cat are due to wear and tear on their organs, as well as on their muscles, ligaments and joints. This is why more frequent veterinary

APPROACHING THE END

It is a commonly told story that cats nearing the end of their lives just disappear, going off on their own to hide away and die. This does appear to be the case for some cats and it is believed that one of the reasons for it is because, in evolutionary terms, being ill and frail would make them easy prey for predators. Hence, by hiding away they are less vulnerable to attack. This is the same reason why cats are very good at hiding signs that they are in pain, as again this would make them more vulnerable to danger of attack. The concern over this situation is that you won't know whether your cat has passed away in pain, or whether they had a peaceful end. This is at least something that you have control over if you choose euthanasia.

health checks (every six to twelve months or so) are important, so that any problems can be picked up and treated early. Constant low-grade pain reduces a cat's quality of life.

Arthritis

Many elderly cats are affected by arthritis – *see* earlier in this chapter.

Dental disease

This can cause cats pain when they are eating, making them salivate, have very bad breath and even paw at their mouths if it is very severe. You may also notice that your cat doesn't groom as well as usual and doesn't want to be touched around the mouth area. Your vet will be able to diagnose dental disease and may suggest a dental procedure to remove the tartar and to scale and polish the teeth, as well as to remove any rotten teeth. This has to be performed under general anaesthesia, but your vet will explain how this can be done most safely in an elderly cat.

Hyperthyroidism

This disease is common amongst older cats and leads to a deterioration in the whole body due to an abnormally high metabolic rate. This means that your cat will appear to be ravenously hungry and yet at the same time as eating a lot, she will also be losing weight. Although an overactive thyroid can potentially be very serious, it can be treated in several ways and the disease can usually be controlled with lifelong medication or an operation.

Heart disease

Just like the rest of the body, the heart can suffer from a lifetime of wear and tear, and older cats can be affected by heart disease. Your vet will check your cat's heart on routine visits and can pick up any problems at an early stage if they see your cat regularly.

Kidney disease

Kidney disease is quite common amongst older cats. Common symptoms include an increase in thirst and sometimes you will also notice weight loss. Although age-related kidney disease cannot be cured, diet and medication can often help to slow down the progression of the disease, allowing patients a longer and better quality of life (*see* earlier in this chapter).

Lumps and bumps and cancer

There is no doubt that cancer is more common in old age. Older cats can develop lumps and bumps on their body that you find as you stroke or groom them. There are many types of cancer and they may not be as obvious as a fast-growing lump that you can readily see or feel. Your vet may need to perform certain diagnostic tests, such as fine needle aspirates or biopsies, in order to diagnose cancer in your cat. How you decide on the right course of action for treatment will vary with every cat and in every different circumstance. In addition to the conventional approaches to treatment, which include chemotherapy, surgery and even radiotherapy, there are also complementary therapies to consider. These can be used either as a sole form of treatment or as part of an integrated approach to care.

Dementia/senility

With more and more cats reaching very advanced ages, more are suffering from dementia or reduced brain function due to ageing. Aggression, confusion and a reduced ability to cope with stress or changes to their routine, as well as increased vocalization and inappropriate urination or defecation, are among some of the signs of dementia in senior cats. Some cats also show signs of memory loss, such as demanding to be fed straight after you have just fed them, as they seem to have forgotten that they have just eaten.

There are certain supplements that can help with brain ageing, as well as the lifestyle factors and adaptations to the home environment that have been covered in this chapter.

6 THE INDOOR CAT

The idea of keeping a cat indoors, without giving them any access to outside, is unthinkable to many people. However, not everyone thinks this way and some cat lovers don't have the option of a feline-friendly outdoor space. There certainly are some circumstances, such as living on busy roads or in high-rise apartments, where it just wouldn't be sensible to allow a cat outside. Indoor cats have special emotional, physical and dietary needs based on their more sedentary lifestyle. This chapter explains how to keep these cats happy and healthy, using a natural approach to everyday care, but the bottom line is that taking the decision to keep a cat indoors only shouldn't be taken lightly. This confined way of life can pose significant risks to a cat's mental,

emotional and physical well-being and so should never be pursued without careful consideration of your cat's best interests.

INDOOR VERSUS OUTDOORS

It can be a tricky decision as to whether you opt to keep your cat indoors all the time or whether she is allowed free access to the outdoors via a cat-flap, for example. Some owners opt for a middle ground whereby they let their cat out for a period of time every day under supervision, whilst others keep their cats in only at night. There are good reasons for each of these options for semi-confinement, and for most cat owners they are not made lightly.

The indoor cat.

Indoors only

For some owners the need to keep a cat as an indoor-only companion will be linked to living in a flat or near a busy road, and perhaps to having lost cats in the past. For others, the decision to keep a cat indoors is related to fear of accidents or injury if they allow them out. Some breeders take the decision to keep their cats indoors because they are extremely valuable, and they feel that it would be too much of a risk to let them out. In general, cats adapt well to an indoor life if that's what they are accustomed to from an early age.

Of course, the majority of cat owners allow their cats to come and go as they choose. After all, they are well known as an independent species and it seems most natural to allow them their freedom.

ADVANTAGES OF KEEPING YOUR CAT INDOORS

- The risk of serious injury is reduced and cats tend to have a longer life expectancy.
- The risk of getting fleas and other parasites such as worms are reduced.
- There is a reduced risk of cat fight injuries.
- Indoor cats often have a closer relationship with their owners.
- There is a lower risk of catching an infectious disease (for example from neighbourhood cats).
- There is a reduced risk of your cat being lost or stolen (especially for pedigrees).
- Your cat will not kill prey, such as songbirds, and bring them into the house. This is better for the wildlife in your neighbourhood and for relationships with your neighbours.

DISADVANTAGES OF KEEPING YOUR CAT INDOORS

- You will have to take responsibility for providing your cat with all the physical and mental stimulation they need in order to stay contented and healthy. Remember, it is an unnatural existence for your cat to be confined to the indoor environment.
- There is an increased risk of your cat suffering from obesity, as she will have a restricted territory and take much less physical exercise.
- Your cat will be more prone to behavioural problems due to the lack of social contact with other cats and due to the frustration and boredom that is common in indoor cats.
- The risk of damage to furniture and carpets through scratching is increased.
- You will need to provide plenty of litter trays.
- You will need to spend time every day engaging, interacting and playing with your cat to help compensate for the lack of outdoor life.
- Lack of street wisdom and good sense if your cat does accidentally get outside leaves them at greater risk of road traffic accidents.
- Stress may potentially be caused by other cats that they might see and/or smell on their territory, through windows or doors.

*Indoor cats
can still find
spots to
sunbathe.*

Outdoor cats

You must make the decision as to whether you want your cat to live 100 per cent indoors or not at an early stage because if kittens get used to going outdoors, it can then be problematic to restrict them to an indoor life later on.

If it is impossible for you to allow your cat to have free access to the outside, perhaps due to where you live, then you will have to consider certain compromises. Your cat may get used to going out under supervision and it can become part of her daily routine. You can make this easier by timing the outdoor visits to be just before mealtimes, so that your cat has an incentive to stay near the house. Every individual is different, though, and you may find that your cat is so independent and active that she strays further than you would like on these 'supervised' sessions. In such cases you may have to decide to give your cat more freedom and accept that she is not suited for a life inside. On the other hand, though, some cats do take to the

indoor life and don't seem that interested in roaming far from their garden on their supervised outings.

One alternative is to fence in your garden, or a part of it, making an enclosure for her so that your cat can go out unsupervised and you know that she won't escape.

Finally, bear in mind that recent research has shown that cats do not usually have a large territory anyway, with most not straying further than a few doors (or fields) away from home.

Safety first

As with any pet, being out in the big wide world can be dangerous for cats. But there are practical ways that you can make life safer for your cat. Firstly, train her to come back inside when you call her. You can do this by first letting her out at around feeding time, so that when she is called back in she is immediately rewarded by food. Another important way of helping to keep your cat safe will be to have her microchipped and attach a visual identity tag to her collar. Make sure that any collar your cat wears has a safety quick-release mechanism in case it gets caught when she is climbing or exploring.

Indoors before dark

Being out at night can be dangerous for your cat as she will be at increased risk of road traffic accidents (cats can be dazzled by car headlights and may freeze in the middle of the road) so make sure that she is wearing a high-visibility reflective collar. Dusk and night time are also the hours when your cat may well have to fight to defend her territory, as cats are naturally most active at these times. So if this is a concern for your cat, it may be best to keep her in at night in order to minimize the potential risk of injury from fighting.

A well-fenced garden is safer for cats.

Of course, if you are keeping your cat indoors at night, don't expect her to stay curled up asleep all night. This is her active time, especially at dusk and dawn; she will be up and about playing and snacking, so make sure that you leave your cat plenty of interactive toys and places to roam in the house. Finally, unless you keep your bedroom door shut, expect to be woken at dawn as your cat asks to be let out or wants to play!

TRANSITION TIME

If your new adult cat has previously led an active outdoor life but now can no longer do so because of where you live, this can be a huge problem and in some cases an insurmountable one. If it is a new cat that you are considering taking on, then if at all possible it is better that she goes to a new home where she can continue to live an outdoor life. Indeed, most rescue centres are careful to match cats to new homes that will provide them with the same type of lifestyle they had previously, and they do not send free-roaming cats to indoor-only homes. Similarly, if you are moving to a place where it will no longer be safe or possible for your cat to have access to the outdoors, you will need to think very carefully about whether she will adapt, or whether she would be happier being re-homed.

Of course, some cats aren't very outdoorsy and others may not want to go outside much in their old age, in which cases these cats may well adapt to an indoor lifestyle later in life.

For young, active cats, however, such a change can be highly distressing, as they will not be used to a life in relative captivity. In trying to adapt to an indoor life, these cats may develop behaviour problems such as becoming destructive and

Some cats aren't very outdoorsy.

they were brought up in, and whether they have been well socialized or not. Cats that are best suited to a life indoors will have been born and brought up in an indoors-only environment. In addition, as a general rule there are certain breeds that may fare better with a life indoors than others; these include the Ragdoll and the Persian.

Ragdoll cats are known for their gentle and tolerant natures and are believed to require less exercise and space than other breeds and to be relatively uninterested in hunting. They are thought to be good house cats as they are usually less interested in going outside than other breeds. Persians, with their characteristic flat faces and long, fine coats, are affectionate and companionable. They are thought to be as happy to be indoors as out and are an easy-going breed.

aggressive, purely due to frustration and 'cabin fever'. These cats need much more attention in terms of interactive play and activities, using toys and climbing frames for instance, to keep them mentally and physically challenged. Cats adapting to an indoor lifestyle, especially after being active and outdoors, also need to have smaller meals to avoid them getting fat.

BREED PERSONALITIES

Are certain breeds of cat more suited to a life indoors? Whilst selective breeding has created a range of pedigree cats that display certain characteristics and specific personality traits, there are other factors than breed alone that define how your cat behaves. These include their background and what kind of environment

SPECIAL NEEDS OF THE HOUSE CAT

For an active animal like the cat, an indoor environment can quickly become predictable and boring, and this can lead to stress, inactivity and obesity. This is why careful attention to your indoor-only cat's home environment is crucial. You need to provide her with everything that she would have found outside, and more!

Back to basics
Of course, just like cats that can come and go, your indoor-only cat will need one or more litter trays (one on each floor of the house). She will need a full complement of beds and resting places, some in high places and others in quiet places, all out of the way of draughts and some with hoods for privacy. She will also need food and water bowls in a variety of places around the house – but never near her toilet area.

CATNAPPING

One thing that cats are well known for is sleeping. In fact, cats can spend up to eighteen hours a day resting and sleeping. The purpose of this downtime was originally to allow your cat to conserve energy for the short but intense bursts of activity involved in catching prey. Of course, with domestic cats being fed by us, this sleeping time is now less crucial for survival. Cats usually sleep in one of two positions, either crouching in an upright position with their paws tucked underneath them, or lying on their sides with their body curled around and their tail tucked in. Even though they may look fast asleep, cats are usually still alert and ready for action at the slightest sound.

Home sweet home

Territory is just as important for indoor cats as it is for those that can come and go in the outside world. The only difference is that for indoor cats their territory has been artificially condensed down into the house and indoor spaces only, so it is much more restricted than most cats would naturally prefer. This space is made even tighter when there is more than one cat in the household, so for an indoor cat a multiple-cat household holds even more potential problems.

As the house will be your cat's sole territory, it is understandable that any changes in your home, either physically, visually or in terms of noise or scent, will have a bigger impact on her than it would if she could go outdoors as well. This is why it is important to keep the home environment as familiar as possible and to ensure that your cat has a place to escape to if you, for

Catnapping.

Sleeping on home territory, completely relaxed.

example, have a lot of visitors over and the house becomes busy and noisy!

Another important aspect of your cat's territory is the fact that cats prefer to do certain things in certain places. This means that she will have a particular spot where she eats, and another completely separate area where she uses the toilet and where her litter tray should be positioned. Yet another area may be where your cat likes to sunbathe and in another elevated position is where she'll enjoy being able to survey her territory with ease. Understanding what your cat does where, and why, are crucial aspects of appreciating the feline psyche and help to explain why you mustn't put her litter tray near her feeding area or move her favourite beds around!

Smells like home
Be conscious of the fact that your cat lives in a world dominated by scent and she will have left scent marks all around her territory (your home) to make herself feel safe, secure and happy. Overly vigorous cleaning that removes all the reassuring odours your cat has left by rubbing and bunting (this is the term used when your cat rubs her face on things) can therefore upset her. So be conservative with your house-cleaning routine, especially at cat head-height, such as around skirting

---

REDUCING STRESS FOR YOUR INDOOR CAT

As the indoor environment is your cat's whole world she can get easily upset or stressed when new things arrive in it. These new things can be as seemingly innocuous as shopping bags, but to your cat they will be loaded with unfamiliar and potentially alarming scents. You can help to combat any such stress by putting shopping away in cupboards straight away and covering any foreign-smelling bags or other items with a blanket or an old towel that has your cat's own familiar scent on it.

---

boards and at the base of kitchen units and furniture.

Take extra care when you return from visiting cat-owning friends because you will come home smelling of their cats (so change your clothes before you greet your cat). Your own resident moggie can detect a foreign scent a mile off and may think that other cats have invaded her home turf, which is another potential source of stress and anxiety for your indoor cat.

Looks like home

As your indoor cat doesn't have access to trees or fences to flex, tone and wear down her claws, you will need to provide her with the best in the way of scratching posts. Cats prefer natural fibre coverings with a vertical thread down which they can rake their claws, keeping them in good shape, as well as being a means of leaving important scent marks. This scent comes from the glands on the underside of your cat's paws, between her footpads. Cats also use scratching posts to leave a visual signal to mark their territory, as well as an auditory reminder of their presence.

Provide climbing centres and scratching posts for indoor cats.

A strong, stable post that is tall enough for your cat to be able to stretch out fully using her front claws at the top of the post is best. Be aware that many scratching posts on the market are just too short and too flimsy. You will need a few of these posts at various locations around the house, as well as some horizontal scratching pads as some cats prefer these. Try them out in different locations but understand that your cat will be likely to use them most if they are in places that she regards as important parts of her territory or in places where she feels vulnerable and wants to assert her presence. Try them out in places such as the landing, by outside doors or at the bottom of the stairs.

Play and socializing

Just because your cat isn't going outside where she would have had access to gardens and potentially to fields and farmland, it doesn't mean that your cat can't engage in her innate hunting behaviour. A cat's ingrained hunting sequence consists of four stages: watching, stalking, chasing and pouncing (and sometimes killing). Even indoor cats will still have this in-built instinct to hunt, so you must engage and stimulate them with suitable toys and games to mimic these instinctive behaviour patterns. If you don't, then it is likely that your carpets, armchairs and upholstery, as well as sometimes your bare ankles or hands, will suffer, as your cat has to find other outlets for her energy and hunting instincts.

Cats go through the motions of hunting many times every day (even if they are not catching prey), using toys, string or balls of waste paper or anything else that they can find that is light and fast moving. You can help to keep an indoor cat happy by instigating and responding to hunting, chasing and pouncing games with them

Indoor cats need to play.

putting on weight unless you keep an eye on how much and what you are feeding them. In addition, keeping fit and active is incredibly important for the indoor cat because a sedentary life is just too easy when there's no going out. In fact obesity and an indoor lifestyle have been linked to conditions such as lower urinary tract

on a daily basis. A further benefit of play is the opportunities it offers for bonding and social interaction, which are vitally important for an indoor cat, as you and other family members are a large part of their world.

Toys
These don't have to be expensive: think how entertaining a cardboard toilet roll, a scrunched-up paper bag or a laser pointer can be for your cat. Many commercial cat toys are designed more to attract owners than to interest their pets. Cats are hard-wired to play with their prey, so it is not surprising that they enjoy pouncing, stalking and swiping at small, fast-moving objects. You can substitute corks, balls of paper, toilet rolls and feathers on a string for a real mouse! Maintain a degree of novelty for your cat by changing the toys that you use and have available for her to play with, as this will keep your cat engaged and inquisitive.

Dietary requirements and keeping fit
Indoor-only cats usually expend far less energy on a daily basis than their outdoor cousins and so are at greater risk of

---

HOW TO SPOT SIGNS OF STRESS IN YOUR INDOOR CAT

Signs that your cat may be bored or frustrated with their indoor-only environment may become apparent with any of the following symptoms or behaviours:

- Increased amount of time sleeping.
- Lack of interest in play/interaction/ food or any change to their usual temperament.
- Attacking or aggressive behaviour towards you, such as biting and scratching.
- Inappropriate urination or defecation, not using the litter trays.
- Urine spraying.
- Over-grooming or constant licking at areas of their body.

If you have any doubts about your cat's mental or physical health have her checked over by your vet. If the problem is found to be linked to or caused by the constraints of the indoor lifestyle then this is the most crucial thing to attend to in order to achieve a lasting solution. As a matter of urgency you must enrich your cat's environment and make her feel safe and secure in her home.

disease and behavioural problems associated with frustration.

There is a wide range of commercially produced diets especially formulated for indoor cats. These have a lower calorie content than other foods and some veterinary diets may also contain a controlled balance of minerals to potentially reduce the risk of urinary tract problems. Make sure that you accurately weigh out your cat's daily rations of food to ensure that you are not over-feeding her. Also be aware that you are not feeding your cat as a substitute for giving her affection or playing with her; read the signals and don't think that your cat is always after food!

Playtime and using interactive feeding methods where you hide small amounts of dry kibble around the house for your cat to search out are a good way of keeping her active and mentally switched on. Similarly, you can buy commercial 'puzzle feeders' that do the same job and can be a great way of keeping your indoor cat fruitfully occupied.

The size of your house and how much your cat gets around it will have a significant impact on her fitness level. If you have a large home over several floors, then you can encourage your cat to move around to different areas by playing games that span the whole house. You can also encourage your cat to use various different parts of the house by having her favourite beds and resting places located on different floors, so that she has to climb stairs to reach them.

Finally, encourage your indoor cat to increase her water intake, as a sedentary, indoor lifestyle has been linked to an increased risk of the development of urinary tract problems. Use water fountains and a range of wide-brimmed water bowls around the house and don't forget

Some indoor cats are allowed outside, if supervised.

that some cats like to drink from a dripping tap.

ENRICHING THE ENVIRONMENT

Enriching your indoor cat's environment means ensuring that her territory (your home), provides her with plenty of opportunities to exercise all her natural behaviours, such as climbing, exploring, 'hanging out' and hiding. In other words, you need to pay special attention to providing your cat with the means of getting enough mental and physical stimulation, just through being indoors, to keep her contented and physically healthy. This means that you will need to either buy or make climbing areas and platforms for your cat, as well as providing her with a range of toys (more than you would need for a cat that can go outside as well), and set aside time every day to play and engage with your cat. This can turn out to be both more expensive as well as more time-consuming than if you were to have cats that could go outside and entertain themselves.

Remember that because your cat will not have the freedom to interact with a range of people or other animals, or with the interesting and exciting environment outside, you will become her main social companion and means of excitement. One of the main problems affecting indoor-only cats is that they become bored and frustrated, as well as overweight. To remedy this and keep your cat content, you will need to make plenty of time to interact with her, and she shouldn't be left alone for long periods during the day. This is one of the reasons why this lifestyle would not be an appropriate or fair choice for people who are out at work all day, and would be better suited to those who work from home or are retired.

HAIRBALLS

Some cats, especially long-haired breeds, suffer from hairballs (also called fur-balls). This is when hair accumulates in their stomach but, rather than passing through the digestive system, it is brought back up and regurgitated. An occasional hairball is quite normal, but frequent regurgitation needs attention. You can help to prevent hairballs by regularly grooming your cat to help remove excessive hair. Many cats self-medicate by chewing on grass to help them to regurgitate hairballs.

An indoor garden

Bring the outdoors inside and give your cat catnip and 'cat grass', such as alfalfa, wheat grass and oat grass. 'Cat grass' is the name used to describe a number of different types of grass that are popu-

Provide 'cat grass' for indoor cats.

lar with cats. The two main species are *Dactylis glomerata* (also called Cock's foot or Orchard grass), and *Avena sativa* (common oat or cat oat). Other common types of grass often referred to and sold as 'cat grass' include barley and wheatgrass. Whichever type you choose, always make sure that you keep it cut so that it does not grow to form awns, which are the spiky tips produced by some grasses (including oats) when they have gone to seed. These can be dangerous for your cat to ingest.

It is still not known why cats eat grass, but we do know that in the natural world when cats eat their prey, they also ingest the prey's stomach contents. This contains small amounts of plant material. So it may be that non-hunting indoor cats are mimicking this in-built behaviour.

Chewing grass provides your cat with a source of fibre, supporting a healthy digestion, and can help with the passage of hairballs through the system or allow them to be regurgitated more easily. It is also believed that some cats like the sweet taste of the grass and enjoy chewing it. It may also provide her with certain vitamins and minerals that she may not get elsewhere in her diet. Finally, chewing on grasses is part of your cat's natural repertoire of behaviours and will be a key addition to her 'enriched' home environment.

Providing dedicated grass and catnip for your cat will also help to prevent your cat from nibbling at other indoor plants that are less well suited to her (*see below*). Most pet shops sell a selection of 'cat grasses' which can be either grown from seed or bought fully grown.

Cats and poisonous plants

Whilst catnip and cat grass can be beneficial for your cat, take great care when

---

LETHAL LILIES

Many houseplants are poisonous to cats, none more so than the Lily. All parts of the lily are highly toxic to cats and can cause kidney failure and death within three to seven days of exposure. Prevention is better than cure, so keep all lily arrangements well out of your cat's reach, or better still, do not have them in the house at all. Even nibbling a lily leaf, licking pollen off their coat or drinking the water from a vase of lilies can be fatal for your cat. In any case of suspected poisoning, take your cat to the vet immediately. Never 'watch and wait'.

---

choosing other houseplants. Most cats are fastidious and careful about what they eat, but boredom can play a part for your indoor cat and she may turn to houseplants as a source of inspiration. Cats that have free access to the outside world tend to ignore houseplants as they have other things to occupy their minds than sampling unfamiliar household greenery.

The following common houseplants are potentially poisonous for cats. The majority taste bad, so would not ordinarily be eaten. However, it is better to be safe than sorry, so avoid having the following in the house, especially if you have an indoors-only cat: amaryllis, chrysanthemum, cyclamen, elephant's ear, ferns, hyacinthus, senecio and umbrella plant. (Do bear in mind that this list is by no means exhaustive.)

A room with a view

Cats certainly need access to daylight, so resting places on windowsills where your cat gets a good view of the world outside can be rewarding as well as healthy. Although supplying an interesting and changing outlook, whether urban or rural, will usually be a great bonus for the indoor cat, always ensure that they are not distressed or upset by anything that is going on outside. Sometimes the sight of neighbourhood cats can be unsettling for an indoor cat as they can't go out and see them off! Always make sure that the windows your cat likes watching from are securely shut and that your cat is not in danger of falling from them.

Conversely, although cats like to be able to observe the world and see what is going on outside, it does not work so favourably the other way around. Cats generally hate to be stared at and could find it highly stressful in ground-floor rooms, for example, to be observed by cats on the outside, through the window or patio doors. Make your indoor cat feel more secure by breaking up her view of others in such situations by using furniture or other barriers as a screen.

Accessories and extras for the indoor cat
You can buy a wide range of accessories to help make life for your indoor cat as stimulating, rewarding and secure for her as possible. These range from specially designed screens to hide her from the possible attentions of neighbourhood cats who may stare in through the windows, to climbing units and high-level beds. You can also buy water fountains to encourage your cat to drink, as they often prefer to lap from running water. In addition, there is a range of toys, such as feathers on a string, squeaky mice, catnip-stuffed shapes and puzzle feeders, that can help to keep her occupied. You may also need to invest in a greater range of different beds (such as covered

Indoor cats can find it stressful to be stared at through the windows.

igloo-style ones), litter trays and grooming equipment (such as nail clippers) than you would do for a cat that has access to the outdoors.

Walking on a harness
If you want to give your indoor cat a taste of the outdoors, then you can train her to wear a harness and take her out on a lead. Walking with a harness can be a compromise for those owners who feel the outdoors is too risky for their cat and yet want to give them the chance to go outside. Not all cats take to wearing a harness, but most relaxed, confident individuals can be gradually introduced to wearing one and then to having a lead attached.

Whichever harness you choose, it must be comfortable and escape-proof. You should be able to fit one finger's width under the straps at any point. If it is too tight it will be uncomfortable, but if it is too loose your cat will wriggle out of it. Allow your cat to get used to wearing her harness in the house before attempting to attach a lead and take her outside.

Start lead training inside. It should not take long for your cat to get used to you holding the end of the lead. Once she is happy with the feel of the slight tension when you hold the lead, take her outside to an area where she can feel secure and confident, and try a short lead walk there. Unlike with a dog, using a lead with a cat is only for safety, so do not pull on it or try to use it to make her go where you want. Only take your cat to private, enclosed, quiet places, preferably your own garden or a communal garden for apartments, for example. Avoid parks and any possible contact with dogs or potentially frightening experiences such as loud noises or busy roads.

Finally, do not start lead walking out-doors with your cat unless you will be able to do it regularly. It is unfair to introduce her to a potentially exciting and rewarding environment, and then to deny her access to it.

COPING WITH CHANGES TO THE INDOOR ENVIRONMENT

We know that cats thrive on predictability and having everything about their home environment the same at all times, but what happens if you want to redesign your kitchen, for example? Or re-do the spare room? Will it cause too much emotional upheaval for your house cat? It is true that redecorating and home improvements do often cause significant stress for indoor-only cats, and this is a common time for problem behaviours such as spraying and inappropriate elimination to start happening. However, by taking care and making appropriate provision for your cat at these times, and ensuring that she has different coping strategies available to her, making changes to the layout of the house, changing the furniture or redecorating shouldn't cause her undue anxiety.

Make sure that at every stage in any redecorating process your cat has a quiet and familiar sanctuary to retreat to. Help to preserve continuity in the scent and feel of your home by tackling building work step by step. In situations where noise, builders and hazards are likely to overtake your cat's entire territory, then it may be preferable to consider sending her to a cattery for the duration of the work.

Visitors
Having new people visiting the house is yet another potential stressor for your cat. How she copes depends on her personality, as well as on the visitor. Some

Some cats retreat when there are visitors in the house.

cats will take to the fuss and attention that they may receive, whilst others are very timid and find this highly stressful.

To make your cat feel safe and secure when people visit, always make sure that she has a place to retreat to, such as a spare room or a study. Ensure that there is food and water available here and that your cat can still reach her other essential resources, such as the litter tray, without having to engage with any visitors. If your cat is very timid and easily stressed by strangers, give her access to plenty of hiding places so that she can simply get out of the way of the action and watch from a safe distance.

Hands-off interactive toys, such as a feather on a string, are an ideal means for an unfamiliar individual to try to bond with your cat. It gives your cat the opportunity to be in control, coming out to play if she wants to or staying safely hidden if she doesn't, and is a good way of introducing regular visitors and friends to your cat.

HOW TO COPE WITH ALLERGIES TO CATS

Having an indoor cat can cause particular problems for owners who have allergies to cats. Symptoms of allergies to cats include those that are similar to the common cold, such as nasal congestion, coughing and itching of the nose and eyes. The allergy is usually due to exposure to one or more allergens produced by cats, commonly the proteins in their saliva. With cats grooming themselves so regularly and marking their scent around the house, exposure to allergens will be widespread in households that have cats. The most fundamental advice is to not keep a cat at all! However, in some instances an allergy develops after you have taken on a cat and in some cases proves not severe enough to warrant re-homing.

There are several measures you can take in order to minimize exposure to cat allergens in the home. These include vigorous and regular hoovering, not having carpets or other soft furnishings in areas that your cats occupy, having designated areas for your cat and parts of the house that are cat-free, as well as regular brushing (preferably done by another member of the household). It is also important to wash your hands after handling cats, if you have an allergy. There is much debate over whether certain breeds or types of cat are less likely to provoke an allergic reaction than others.

7 DIET AND NUTRITION

The importance of your cat's daily diet cannot be underestimated. A nutritious diet is the foundation of good health, without which truly 'holistic' care is not possible.

This chapter will explain how to feed a balanced diet throughout your cat's different life stages. It will also look into the dietary needs of the cat, understanding why, as strict carnivores, they rely on nutrients in animal tissues to meet their specific and unique nutritional requirements. Finally, it will examine how pet foods are manufactured commercially and how to read the labels so that you can make comparisons and choose the most suitable diet to keep your cat fit and healthy.

A BALANCED DIET

You are what you eat. This is as true for cats as it is for us. Therefore your cat's diet is the key to her long-term health, in terms of life expectancy, resistance to disease and overall well-being. Recent research has confirmed that cats will consistently choose a diet that reflects as closely as possible the same level of proteins, carbohydrates and fats that are contained in their natural prey of mice and birds. This is over 50 per cent protein, around a third fat and a very small proportion of carbohydrate. Most good cat foods have a high protein/low carbohydrate ratio, making them a highly palatable and natural diet for cats.

However, it must not be forgotten that

a cat's individual dietary needs depend on their age, state of health and level of activity (such as whether they are indoor or outdoor cats). So no single diet will be right for every cat at every stage of life.

STRICT CARNIVORES

Cats are so highly specialized that they are known as 'hypercarnivores', because through evolution they have developed to thrive on a diet that is almost exclu-

Cats are strict carnivores.

sively based on small mammal prey: mice, voles, rabbits and birds. Therefore cats have strict requirements for certain nutrients that can only be found in meat. They have specific behavioural, anatomical, physiological and metabolic adaptations to reflect this diet and have unique metabolic pathways that allow them to cope with such a high protein diet. In addition, cats have an absolute requirement for certain amino acids (the building blocks of protein), which must be supplied in their diet; these are called 'essential amino acids' and are again found in meat.

Essential amino acids

Cats source more than half their daily calorie intake from protein and have a unique metabolism to reflect this. Adult cats require between two and three times more protein in their diet than adults of omnivorous species such as dogs. They have an absolute requirement for four amino acids in particular, which must be supplied in their diet. These are arginine, taurine, methionine and cystine; all are found in meat and each plays a crucial role in a cat's everyday bodily functions.

Taurine

This 'essential' amino acid is crucial in feline diets because cats, unlike most other mammals, cannot make it from other amino acids that they have in the body. Thus it is essential that cats take in adequate taurine in their diet on a regular basis.

Taurine is an important component of muscles (including the heart), the central nervous system and the retina of the eye. Among its other roles, taurine is also crucial in the formation of bile salts, necessary for the effective digestion of fats in the small intestine. Taurine is found exclusively in meat and animal-based products,

---

UNIQUE NUTRITION

It is well known that you can feed your dog cat food (if you are desperate), but cats should not be fed dog food. This is because cats are obligate carnivores and have a need for certain essential nutrients such as taurine, whereas dogs are omnivores and do not necessarily need a strictly meat diet in order to survive. Cats and dogs have very different nutritional requirements and hence need different types of food.

---

which is why cats, as obligate carnivores, need a diet rich in meat (both muscles and organs).

Prolonged deficiencies of taurine can result in central retinal degeneration, resulting in blindness, as well as dilated cardiomyopathy (DCM). In this condition, the heart dilates, and as its walls become thinner and weaker, heart failure can occur. The potentially serious effects of taurine deficiency are now so well recognized that proprietary cat foods now all contain supplemental taurine, in line with European Federation recommendations.

Other dietary adaptations for the super-carnivore

Another important carnivorous adaptation of the feline digestive system is that cats lack the ability to convert the essential fatty acid linoleic acid (contained in plants) into arachidonic acid (contained in animal fat). Arachidonic acid is essential for blood clotting, reproduction and coat condition, while linoleic acid is vital for growth, liver function and wound

Cats need a meaty diet.

healing. In addition, they cannot convert beta-carotene to vitamin A and require dietary sources of vitamins A and D.

For these reasons cats need to eat a diet that contains meat as the most important constituent. Cats are metabolically adapted to preferentially use protein and fat as energy sources and have little requirement for carbohydrates. In order to cater for their highly specialized nutritional needs most high-quality cat foods will contain added vitamin A as well as taurine to ensure that your cat's particular needs are always met.

TYPES OF DIET

With such a variety of different foods available for your cat it can be difficult to decide on the best choice of diet. The most straightforward and popular choice for most cats is a mixture of commercial wet and dry cat foods, with the emphasis on natural, organic, wet foods. However, some owners like to consider home-cook-ing for their cat, whilst others prefer a raw meaty diet. To help you make your choice, it is also important to appreciate the reasons why dry kibble and carbohy-drate-rich foods are not suited to a cat's digestion and metabolism, and why wet foods may prove a better option.

Choosing a cat food

When buying cat food in a shop, read the label carefully but also try to have a look at the food itself. Ask to see an open bag or can, or better still arrange to take a sample home. Have a close look, smell and feel of the food when you put it out into your cat's bowl.

Do your homework about the company that makes it and arm yourself with enough information so that you know exactly what has gone into your chosen cat food. Where is the meat sourced? Does the food contain grain or other car-bohydrates, and if so how much? And how is the food preserved? Does it con-tain artificial preservatives and additives?

Any ethical, caring pet food company that values its customers will be happy to answer all your questions.

Wet or dry food?

This is the most fundamental question to ask when deciding how to best feed your cat. Dry food is usually prepared by cooking and then drying the food under pressure, and then spraying it with fat to add flavours that enhance palatability. A preservative must then be added to prevent the fat from becoming rancid and to allow the food to have a longer shelf life. Vitamins and minerals are also usually added back to the meat at this point, as all the naturally occurring goodness will have been lost through the lengthy, high temperature industrial processing.

Wet foods, on the other hand, have usually been cooked and then heat-sterilized and sealed into tins or sachets. This type of food does not have to have added preservatives because of the way it has been vacuum-sealed.

The benefits of wet food include the fact that it contains more water (it is between 70 and 80 per cent water) than dry diets do. This means that it will be helping to keep your cat, who is naturally a desert-dwelling species with a low thirst drive, well hydrated. This helps to maintain a healthy urinary tract system, looking after long-term kidney health. Hence a wet diet of tinned, canned or fresh meat can help to ensure a good daily water intake for your cat. In addition, this type of food is often more appealing to cats as it is physically more similar to their natural diet and has a more meaty smell and texture.

Dry cat foods, on the other hand, although useful as a form of food that can more easily be left down for ad-lib feeding, usually contain a high propor-

tion of carbohydrate and are much more calorie dense. Unfortunately, although for us it is a convenient type of food to give a cat, it is not generally the healthiest option in the long term, especially if she is overweight. This is because, as we know, cats are not metabolically adapted to use carbohydrates as a main energy source and have a reduced ability to digest and utilize carbohydrates. Added to this, dry kibble is far more calorie dense than wet diets so the portion sizes needed by most cats are very small.

The high level of carbohydrate in dry cat foods is the result of the fact that the manufacturing process requires starch to help the kibble stick together; it acts rather like glue. In addition, the meat that goes into dry cat food usually needs to be in a 'meal' form, rather than as fresh meat, so that it can be physically made into kibble. Meat meal is generally considered to be less high quality than fresh meat and less readily digestible and nutritious as a constituent of pet food.

For these reasons – the lower water content, the higher carbohydrate load and the calorie density – dry diets may not be as healthy as a sole wet diet in the long term. It may be wiser to opt for a fifty/fifty approach or a wet only diet.

One of the benefits of dry food is that it is said to help keep your cat's teeth clean. Indeed, there are some specific dry cat foods for dental health that show some benefits in helping to keep your cat's teeth clean and tartar free. However, regular dry kibble only provides a minor mechanical benefit and cats can still develop dental disease when fed such food. The best way of ensuring that your cat has pearly white teeth and healthy gums will be to get her used to eating raw bones from an early age. (This does, however, carry the potential risks outlined below, concerning the feeding of raw meat diets.) Teaching your cat to tolerate having her teeth brushed is another way of helping to reduce tartar and keep the teeth healthy (ask your vet to give you a demonstration).

Finally, however, do be aware that food preferences in terms of wet or dry food can be hard to alter in cats that have been used to eating a certain type of food. In such cases you will be mainly guided by what your cat is used to, and you may have less of a choice over what you can offer her than you thought!

Grain-free foods

One dietary factor that has been receiving increased attention in obese cats in particular is the role of carbohydrate-rich diets. This may mean that choosing a grain-free diet, such as a wet food or certain new types of kibble that have been baked rather than gone through the usual extrusion process, has a significant beneficial effect on your cat's health, weight and well-being.

As part of their natural diet cats do not consume carbohydrates such as grains (for example, rice and wheat). In fact, research has shown that cats have minimal ability to digest and utilize carbohydrates in their diet. This is reflected in their lack of salivary amylase (an enzyme that breaks down starch) and in the fact that cats show no taste preference towards sugary foods. Cats obtain their energy from protein and fats (found in meat), rather than from carbohydrates.

'Natural' commercial diets

With growing awareness of some of the shortcomings of mass-produced foods, there is a demand for commercial diets that are more 'natural' and wholesome. This is a burgeoning area of the pet food market.

Food preferences can be difficult to change.

There is currently only one criterion pertaining to natural pet foods where stringent regulations apply, and this concerns 'organically certified' food. To be certain of specific minimum standards in your chosen cat food you must make sure that the bag or can is actually stamped with the symbol of a recognized certification body. In the UK these are most often the Soil Association or the Organic Farmers and Growers Association. Certified organic cat food contains meat derived from higher welfare farms where unnecessary antibiotics and growth promoters are not used. Similarly, the vegetables and fruits will have been grown without the use of synthetic fertilizers, and will not contain genetically modified organisms.

Other terms currently favoured by manufacturers of 'natural' cat foods include 'holistic' and 'species appropriate'. Whilst these hold no weight in terms of minimum standards or regulations, they are usually taken to imply that the food is wholesome and contains unprocessed raw ingredients derived from plant and animal sources in their natural state. Being 'species appropriate' means that the food will reflect as much as possible the natural diet of the cat's wild ancestor, so will therefore be most easily digestible and optimally nutritious for them.

Home-made diets

It can be difficult to ensure that home-produced diets contain everything that a cat needs in terms of essential nutrients, which is why commercially produced cat foods are so popular and widely used.

However, if you are keen to produce a home-made diet for your cat you will need to consult your vet or a veterinary nutritionist in order to ensure that you are following recipes that are complete and balanced and are suitable for your individual cat's needs.

Finally, because meat, vegetables and grains are not the same as whole animal carcasses, dietary supplements are nearly always essential when offering your cat a home-made diet. It is also important to

Home-made diets.

realize that some of the foods that you buy fresh may not be as safe as you think. Unless you opt for organically certified produce, be aware that fruit and vegetables can be contaminated with pesticides, fish with heavy metals, grains with moulds and meats with bacteria.

Raw meat diets

Despite the unfortunate acronym, BARF (which stands for Bones As Raw Food or Biologically Appropriate Raw Food) can be a healthy way to feed your pet. It is based on feeding both raw meat and raw bones, along with a small amount of liquidized vegetables. The benefits include clean, tartar-free teeth and a diet that can be both healthy and most similar to a cat's natural diet. The potential downsides include the risk of food poisoning (to both cat and owner), as well as the hazards of feeding raw bones. In addition to the obvious risk of salmonella bacteria in raw poultry meat, there is the additional risk from the protozoan parasite that causes toxoplasmosis (*see* box).

There is now a growing number of 'BARF diet'-inspired pet food companies that deliver frozen, meal-sized portions to your door, making this way of feeding your cat much easier. However, raw meat diets are not suitable and appropriate for all cats, especially the very young and the very old, or those with underlying health issues or a weak digestion. To thrive on such a diet a cat would usually have to have been brought up on it from an early age.

Vegetarian cat food

It will have become clear by now that as strict carnivores cats simply cannot be vegetarians. A few commercial vegetarian cat foods do exist, and they do contain the essential amino acids that cats

---

FOODBORNE DISEASE RISK

One of the important potential pathogens associated with raw meat includes the protozoan parasite (*Toxoplasma gondii*). This affects cats but can also be passed to humans. In humans the greatest risk is to pregnant women as it can cause developmental problems in the growing foetus. Humans typically contract toxoplasmosis from eating undercooked or raw meat, but it can also be picked up from cat faeces during the weeks after a cat consumes the parasite, for example in raw meat.

---

need. However, this is a highly unnatural diet for cats and one that may not provide them with adequate health and nutrition for the long term.

FEEDING GUIDELINES

The daily feeding habits of cats reflect their innate drive for repeated short bursts of hunting, sleeping and feeding over each twenty-four-hour period. This means that they are typically eating ten to twenty small meals throughout the day and night, rather than just one or two discrete meals. This pattern should be reflected in the way in which we feed our cats, giving them small, frequent meals throughout the day.

The exact amount of food to give your cat will vary depending on the individual food. Follow the guidelines given on the can or bag, but be aware that manufacturers usually over-estimate the recommended daily allowance. Also remember that these guidelines will have been calculated for an 'average' cat, and in reality every cat has a slightly different requirement due to their lifestyle, metabolic rate and health profile, so you will need to assess how they get on and adjust the daily amounts accordingly. If possible, divide the total daily amount into ten to twelve small servings a day, to match your cat's preferred feeding pattern.

Obesity

Although figures vary, it has been estimated that around one in four cats in the UK are overweight or obese. The reasons, in the vast majority of cases, are the same as human obesity: eating too much,

eating the wrong type of food, and not getting enough exercise. It will come as no surprise to learn that these cats are putting greater strain on their hearts and joints, and are more likely to be affected by chronic illnesses such as diabetes and heart disease in later life. Prevent your cat from becoming overweight in the first place by paying attention to what you are feeding her and how much exercise she is getting, and finally by not misinterpreting your cat's cry for attention or to play as a demand for food.

Whilst dry foods can be very economical and easy to feed, and allow you to leave food down for your cat to nibble at ad-hoc throughout the day, they are

Obesity is a common problem.

highly calorie dense compared to wet foods, so are not suitable for a cat that needs to lose weight. The manufacturing process means that dry foods contain a high level of carbohydrate, which cats are not designed to use as an energy fuel. Instead, when faced with an overload of carbohydrate, the cat's body will store the excess as fat.

Many people complain that they only feed their cat a small amount of dry food and yet they are still overweight. But for the same calories you can feed your cat three to four times the same volume of fresh or canned foods. Take particular care with feeding neutered cats, as they have a tendency to become overweight (*see* later in this chapter).

FELINE-FRIENDLY FEEDING

Make mealtimes for your cat more interesting. As well as preventing boredom (especially important for the indoor cat), this will help to combat obesity. You can put small (mouse-meal size) portions of food down in different locations around the house, so that your cat has to search them out, making feeding time stimulating and rewarding.

Several factors are thought to affect your cat's food preferences and these will be inherited as well as learned from early experiences of watching her mother and siblings feeding. In terms of what affects palatability of a food, your cat will be concerned about its appearance, temperature, smell, texture and of course taste. No wonder we sometimes think that cats are fussy creatures!

Temperature
The temperature of a cat's food has a strong influence on its acceptance, with cats showing a marked preference for it

---

CASE STUDY: THE OVERWEIGHT INDOOR CAT

Tibby is a three-year-old indoor tabby cat. Like one in four pets in the UK, she is obese. Her daily exercise consists largely of moving between the bed and the sofa, with an occasional sunbathing session on the windowsill. She was fed a good-quality, complete, dry food from the vet. To help her shed her excess pounds Tibby was gradually changed over to a moist canned food diet. More water means fewer calories. She was also offered her small ration of dry food (it was difficult to wean her off her 'munchies' completely) in a toy that she had to chase and play with to get it to release the food. Steadily, with more exercise and a change to a lower calorie diet, Tibby gradually lost her extra pounds.

---

to be around body temperature, like that of their live prey. A food that is either too cold or too hot, as well as being less palatable, will also be harder for your cat to digest. Make sure that her food is at room temperature before you put it down for her, and never feed it straight from the fridge!

Dietary changes
If you are changing your cat's diet, always do so slowly over a few weeks by gradually substituting the old food with the new. This allows your cat's digestive system to adapt gradually to the new diet and should help to avoid any digestive upsets such as diarrhoea that may be associated with too rapid transitions.

Feeding bowls

Ensure that your cat's food bowl is not plastic, because day after day petrochemicals may leach out into the food. Ceramic bowls are usually best, as stainless steel or metal bowls can be noisy. Cats prefer to eat and drink from shallow saucer-like dishes where their whiskers don't touch the sides. They are also very sensitive to stale food odours and moulds, and may not eat unless their food bowls are kept scrupulously clean.

In multiple-cat households make sure that food (and water) bowls are located in various parts of the house, so that every cat gets the opportunity to access food without competition from other cats.

Keep it simple

Your cat should, whenever possible, be able to have her food without it being adulterated. This usually means without the addition of medications, or similar. Therefore, unless it is absolutely essential that a medicine is given as part of a full meal (ask your vet if this is the case), then it is better to give your cat any medicine she may need in a little separate food, or with a treat. If you add medicine to your cat's main meal, she will be faced with having to eat it with the medicine or to go without. This is obviously not a fair choice for your cat, and may also pave the way for an individual to become a fussy eater.

THE TRUTH ABOUT FUSSY FELINES

Why do cats seem to be such fussy eaters? Why is it that the day you stock up on a dozen cans of the food that your cat has been happily wolfing down for a week, she suddenly refuses to eat it any more?

Scientific research tells us that it is not just contrariness; it is more likely to be a natural mechanism to avoid an unbalanced diet, or similarly a hard-wired drive to seek variety. This could be a natural survival strategy to help the cat to avoid dependence on a single food source, and therefore minimize the risk of depleting a single source of prey. In addition, data suggest that a cat's highly developed sense of taste is due to the fact that they are such obligate meat-eaters. Their taste system is uniquely tuned to allow them to determine whether the meat they are consuming contains all the individual amino acids that they need.

A dedicated feeding station.

Cats can be very fussy eaters!

This helps cats to choose meats that contain a balance of all the protein building blocks they need in order to stay fit and healthy.

Their carnivorous eating habits have made cats averse to the bitter flavours and tastes of plant material, and when ingesting their prey cats usually avoid consuming the entrails. They will usually follow their instincts and pick at cat-grass as they choose, in order to get extra roughage and fibre.

Cats show a marked preference for foods that they had when they were young. It has been found that the type of food a cat is fed during their first six months influences the pattern of their food preferences for life. So, cats accustomed to dry food, for example, may refuse food of a different type later on, if they are not used to it. This is why changing a cat's long-standing feeding habits usually requires patience and should be done very gradually over several weeks.

Cats are very sensitive to stale food odours and moulds and often will not eat unless their bowl is very clean. Due to their highly tuned senses cats will also be very sniffy if you offer them anything but the freshest food, so remember to remove any uneaten food within about half an hour of feeding time. Food straight from the fridge will be too cold for your cat's digestive system to be able to cope with properly and it will also be less palatable for them (there is little stimulating aroma from cold food). In addition, cats don't like to eat and drink in the same area, so keep her water bowl well away from where you usually feed your cat.

Finally, it is also a good idea to make sure that you are feeding your cat in a quiet place where she doesn't feel stressed or anxious due to the presence of other cats or household pets, for example.

Most fussy eaters can be made to eat the food that you are offering them, even if they sometimes need some coaxing (some may even prefer their food slightly warmed). However, this is not always the case and some cats just refuse point-blank to eat certain types, flavours or brands of food – and can quite literally almost starve themselves to death. Unlike dogs, which can fast for a day or so, if a cat goes without eating for twenty-four hours or more they can become very ill. If your cat refuses to eat what you put down for her, you will need to tempt her with a different food until she eats.

If she still refuses to eat, despite being offered her usual preferred food, then a veterinary check-up is necessary.

FEEDING FOR DIFFERENT LIFE-STAGES

As well as what you are feeding her, you also need to consider how much to feed your cat every day. With obesity so commonplace, this is important. Remember that feeding guidelines on labels, or other recommendations such as diet sheets or recipes, will be for the average cat of a given size or weight. Thus they do not take into account individual factors such as age, breed, metabolism, activity level and state of health. Each of these factors can affect how much you need to feed your cat, and it may well vary from the average. You may need to seek advice about feeding your cat in particular circumstances such as pregnancy, or for greater or reduced levels of activity.

Kittens

Kittens need to be fed a diet that has been specially formulated for growth, so it is important to choose a food that is labelled as being 'for kittens'. From weaning, kittens still need several small meals throughout the day, as they have smaller

Kittens need a special diet for growth.

stomachs and higher metabolism than adults. Their diet will usually contain a higher percentage of protein to support growth and development and is usually fed until kittens reach maturity at around one year old.

Cats' food preferences are established early in life. By offering your kitten a mixture of wet and dry foods in a range of different flavours you will be broadening her palate so that she is more likely to accept a wide variety of food types as an adult.

Senior cats

A senior diet should reflect an elderly cat's specific needs by containing high-quality ingredients that are easily digestible and rich in nutrients and vitamins. Senior diets are usually fed from the age of about seven to ten onwards. This diet should contain fewer toxins, putting less strain on the liver and kidneys, and thus easing the ageing body's workload (so choose organic or natural diets where possible). Because the senior diet is usually more energy and nutrient dense, it can be fed in smaller quantities, to match the reduced appetite of the older cat. Your cat's digestive system will also become more sensitive as she gets older, making it particularly important not to make any abrupt changes or to offer her anything new for risk of tummy upsets. The more additives and complex unnatural ingredients in the food, the greater will be the workload on your cat's digestive system.

Whilst some cats tend to put on weight as they get older and less active, others have the opposite problem and become very thin as they age. This means that you need to be aware of your senior cat's weight and appetite, and tailor your care and her diet to her individual needs.

Common to all senior cats diets, though, is the need for it to contain higher levels of antioxidants and vitamins that help to protect their ageing bodies from the damaging effects of free radicals.

Feeding the pregnant cat

Every queen is different, but as a general guide it is suggested that the amount of food she receives should be gradually increased from the second week of gestation until parturition (birth). At the end of gestation the queen should be receiving approximately 25 to 50 per cent more food than her normal maintenance needs.

Neutered cats

Neutered cats, especially those kept exclusively indoors, have a tendency to put on weight. This is due to the fact that neutered male and female cats require an estimated 20 per cent fewer calories for their daily maintenance needs, although they tend to eat more as they are more interested in food than they were previously. This is why special diets for neutered cats have been developed that are less calorie dense than regular foods.

The indoor versus the outdoor cat

Indoor cats usually have a less active lifestyle than their outdoor contemporaries, so may need slightly less food on a daily basis in order to prevent obesity.

THE PET FOOD INDUSTRY

The supply of pet food is now a global industry. In 2008 the value of the UK pet food market alone was just under two billion pounds. Commercially produced pet foods have been a booming industry since the Second World War, when mass production first began. It quickly became

Home-made diets are very different from commercial pet foods.

popular with pet owners as people saw how easily they could feed their pets 'all in one' meals from a can. Before this, they would have fed them raw or cooked meat and vegetables, together with scraps from the table, and most cats would have fended for themselves by hunting. It was great for the manufacturers too, who were suddenly able to make leftover by-products into saleable goods.

Of course, in such a huge industry there is wide variation in the way that pet food is manufactured commercially, ranging from small 'kitchen-table' producers using good quality 'real' meat to the mass-market industry where millions of cans run off production lines all over the world every second. In terms of nutritional value and health-giving properties, the differences are as vast as the scale and method of manufacture. You need to do your homework and research the food you are offering your cat, as well as trust your instincts when you see and smell what you are putting into her bowl each day and how it suits her.

What goes into most cat food?
Firstly, let's look at the meat that goes into most supermarket cat foods. The majority is labelled as 'meat and animal derivatives'. According to animal feed legislation, this is meat that is surplus to human consumption or not normally consumed by people in this country, but is passed as 'fit for human consumption'. This information would probably lead you to the interpretation that it is just left-over meat, perfectly edible, but which we either have too much of or we don't usually consume. What you might not imagine is that this meat, classified as 'animal by-products', is stuff that we would never contemplate eating: feathers, hair, hooves, eyes, and so on. This is why the term 'fit for human consumption' in the original statement is somewhat misleading, as 'fit' simply means that the material is free of transmissible diseases and does not derive from sick animals or those that have died naturally. These 'meat and animal derivatives' need to somehow end up as tasty pet food. This is usually done via a process of slow cooking called rendering. Rendered meat can be from any source, any animal and almost any part of it; the label will just say 'meat and bone meal' or 'meat and animal derivatives'. Manufacturers must, of course, ensure that their foods are 'complete and balanced'. How they manage to do this, though, can be quite extraordinary. For example, grains such as corn or rice are used as cheap sources of protein, and as fillers in place of meat. Of course, being so high in grains, these processed diets do not mirror the natural feline diet and what would be nutritionally best for your cat.

Understanding the label
The Food Standards Agency is responsible for the labelling of farm animal food because it is part of the human food chain. Pet food, however, has far less in-

Pet food labelling

Choosing a good-quality cat food can be tricky. The list below should give you some pointers as to what to look out for and, more importantly, what to avoid when reading the ingredient list.

Choose	Avoid
Named meat source (e.g. 60% lamb)	Any use of the words 'derivatives' or 'by-products', such as 'meat & animal derivatives' or 'chicken by-products'
Named meat source (not 'meal' and no 'derivatives', just good old-fashioned real meat!)	'Meal' (e.g. chicken meal)
Wet foods (e.g. canned or foil pouches) for cats	Dry foods for cats as their sole type of diet
As a main food source, choose a 'complete' rather than a 'complementary' food	Feeding 'complementary' or treat foods as the main diet
Natural preservative antioxidants such as mixed tocopherals and rosemary	Preservatives marked as 'EC permitted antioxidants'

formation on its labels, and comes under the jurisdiction of local Trading Standards. Therefore, whilst you can find out the details of what goes into a cow's food, the same is not true for that of your cat. However, regulations do require there to be a statutory statement on every label on every commercially available cat food that must give the name and address of the manufacturer, packer, importer, seller or distributor, and must contain the following obligatory declarations:

Product description: this will indicate whether it is a 'complete' food or a 'complementary' food (such as treats or a mixer), together with which species it is for and directions for feeding.

Typical analysis: the percentage of the following must be listed: proteins, oils and fats, fibre, moisture content (if it is over 14 per cent) and ash. (Ash represents the mineral content of the food, and is determined by burning the product, hence it is termed ash content.)

Ingredients list: every ingredient must be listed, in descending order by amount. They can either be indicated by their category, such as 'meat and animal derivatives' or 'cereal', or by their own individual names. This is up to the manufacturer.

Additives: if preservatives, antioxidants or colours have been added to the product, their presence has to be declared by using the category or chemical name of the additive. Be aware that the term 'EC permitted additives' contains a possible four thousand chemicals, many of which have been banned from human foods.

Vitamins: if vitamins A, D or E have been added, their presence and level must be declared. The level must include the quantity naturally present in the food.

Best before date and net weight must also be stated on the label.

Additives

It is hardly surprising that hyperactivity and other behavioural problems are so often linked to diet. Simply changing to a food that is additive-free will usually make an enormous difference to your cat. These additives are the 'necessary evils' of the manufacturing process to ensure that the food ends up being tasty, appetising and able to stay fresh for months or years. They include emulsifiers, lubricants, anticaking agents, drying agents, thickeners, colourings, sweeteners, animal digest, flavourings, texturizers and grease, and so on. In addition to the harmful effects of these additives by themselves, when added together the effect is relatively unknown.

It is always important to read the label.

WHY DO CATS HAVE SUCH ROUGH TONGUES?

Your cat's tongue does several important jobs. It is covered with hook-shaped barbs that act like a comb when she grooms herself to remove dead fur and debris and keep the coat in perfect condition. The tongue also, of course, allows your cat to taste her food, as well as being spoon-shaped to allow her to lap up water.

WATER

Having fresh water available for your cat at all times is vital, even if you hardly notice her drinking much. Bottled water has been linked to health concerns connected to the leaching of plastics, and environmental damage. Filtered water is a good option for the many cats who are reluctant to drink tap water (they can taste the impurities and treatments).

In addition, cats prefer to drink from wide, shallow dishes, as they don't like their whiskers to touch the sides. They also like to be able to see the meniscus (the surface) at the top of the water in order to help them to judge their distance from it. So always offer your cat water in a wide, shallow, clean ceramic bowl full to the brim and change it at least daily. Make sure that your cat always has access to her water bowls, and that you have plenty of them around the house in a variety of different types of container.

Many cats prefer to drink from running water, so consider using a water fountain (these are commercially available) as a better alternative to a constantly dripping tap.

There is no telling what your cat may prefer to drink from!

PUTTING IT ALL TOGETHER

However you choose to feed your cat, the type of food and the quality of the ingredients, as well as ensuring she has a balanced diet appropriate for her digestive system, are the key factors to consider. This is crucial. But it is also important to assess whether what you are feeding her actually suits your cat's individual constitution and condition. Is she a stay-at-home house-cat or an out-all-day mouser? Not every way of feeding, every recipe or every brand of food brings out the best in every animal. This is down to the individual differences between cats relating to age, breed, metabolic rate and constitutional factors.

Also remember to bear in mind your cat's unique and preferred natural feeding patterns. This means that you should try to simulate her natural pattern of eating by offering ten to twelve 'mouse-size' portions of food a day, rather than the traditional one or two large meals. If you can manage this logistically and practically, it will be a much healthier and more natural way of feeding your cat.

Finally, it is crucial to assess how your cat's diet suits her and keeps her fit and healthy. Pay attention to how she looks and acts. How much energy does she have? How does she behave? What is her coat like? Is it shiny and glossy or dry and dull? How are your cat's stools? How much water does she drink? Is her weight stable and appropriate for her size? How do her teeth look? Is she suffering from tartar build-up and sore gums? Is she in optimum health or suffering from chronic health issues? The answers to each of these questions will be key pointers in helping you to decide whether your cat's diet is the best for her. Diet is the cornerstone of health and therefore needs to be the first thing that you address in any aspect of basic healthcare or healing.

KEEP FOOD AND WATER BOWLS SEPARATE FROM ONE ANOTHER

Cats do not like to eat and drink in the same area, so keep water bowls well away from feeding areas. Hence, double bowls where you can put food right next to water are a real no-no.

8 ROUTINE HEALTH CARE AND COMMONLY USED SUPPLEMENTS

This chapter looks at all the important preventive health care treatments and procedures for your cat, including vaccination, worming, flea treatments and neutering. It will explore why these are necessary and whether complementary treatments would be a suitable alternative. It also takes an in-depth look at the most popular health supplements available for cats.

VACCINATION

Vaccination is one of the most commonly performed procedures in veterinary practice, with millions of cats being vaccinated every year. Widespread vaccination has helped to substantially reduce the impact of several very serious feline diseases on the UK cat population. A vaccine works by stimulating the immune system so that it contains a blueprint of how to respond effectively should it be exposed to a given infection again in the future. So as not to actually cause disease in the cat, vaccines carry a modified or inactivated version of the infectious agent. Vaccination is the number one reason for cats to visit the vet and is usually combined with an annual health check.

Vaccines can generally be divided into those that are essential, so-called 'core vaccines', and those that are only given to certain cats in certain circumstances, so-called 'non-core vaccines'. Core vaccines protect against especially severe or life-

Routine health care is important.

threatening diseases that are widespread in the cat population.

Always speak to your vet about which vaccines will be most beneficial for your cat, based on her particular lifestyle and circumstances. This may vary depending on whether your cat is indoor-only or outdoors, as well as in which part of the country you live and which diseases are most common in your area.

Core vaccines
The following list describes commonly used core vaccines:

Feline panleukopenia virus (FPV, also called feline infectious enteritis or feline parvovirus)
This causes severe haemorrhagic gastro-enteritis, resulting in vomiting and diarrhoea that can prove fatal, especially in kittens. It is highly contagious and can survive for long periods in the environment. Vaccination is highly effective at protecting cats against this disease.

Feline herpesvirus (FHV-1) and feline calicivirus (FCV)
These two viruses are the main agents of 'cat flu' and are combined together in a vaccine. Cats affected by either of these two viruses typically present with signs of sneezing, nasal discharge and conjunctivitis, and may also have mouth ulcers. Symptoms can vary from relatively mild to severe, and can even result in pneumonia. Cats infected with feline herpesvirus (FHV-1) can remain permanently infected (becoming carriers of the virus), suffering from recurring eye infections (and other respiratory symptoms) at intervals throughout their lives.

Both of these respiratory viruses are ubiquitous in the cat population and are usually transmitted by direct contact

---

> **WHAT TO DO IF YOU HAVE A CAT THAT IS POSITIVE FOR FELINE LEUKAEMIA VIRUS?**
>
> Cats identified (via a blood test) as being infected should be isolated from other cats in the household and should become indoor-only cats. You will also need to take measures to ensure that they do not share any food or water bowls or litter trays with other cats in the household. Speak to your vet about any suitable supportive treatments.

---

between infected cats (such as via sneezing) and may also survive in the environment for short periods. Vaccination protects cats from severe cat flu, but does not prevent infection.

Feline leukaemia virus (FeLV)
This is an important disease and so is often considered as a core vaccine, especially for cats that go outdoors. It is a fragile virus that is spread via saliva through prolonged close contact between cats (such as via shared food and water bowls, by mutual grooming or via cat bites). It causes a wide variety of problems in affected cats, including a suppressed immune system, anaemia and lymphoma (a type of cancer), with most cats dying within about three years of being diagnosed.

Non-core vaccines
Non-core vaccines include the following.

Rabies
Some cats may require a vaccination against rabies, for example if they are travelling abroad. Rabies is more common in dogs but can also affect cats and humans (if bitten by an infected animal).

It affects the central nervous system and is fatal.

Chlamydophila felis
This is a type of bacteria that can cause conjunctivitis in cats. The vaccine is usually only used for cats kept in breeding colonies or large groups where there are persistent infections.

Bordatella bronchiseptica
This is another bacteria that can form part of the cat flu complex of infective organisms. Vaccination is not usually considered unless your cat suffers persistent respiratory infections and is part of a large group where there are repeated outbreaks of disease.

Feline Immunodeficiency virus (FIV)
This is quite a common virus affecting outdoor cats and is mainly spread via saliva through bites inflicted during cat fights. At the present time vaccination against this virus is not common in the UK due to the lack of an effective vaccine covering all the different strains of virus.

When do we vaccinate cats?
All kittens should receive their core-vaccines (and any other vaccines that your vet recommends) at around eight to nine weeks of age, with a second injection between three and four weeks later. This is known as their 'primary course' of vaccinations. In some cases your vet may also suggest a third injection at around sixteen to twenty weeks of age, to offer even better protection.

Vaccinations are usually given by injection into the scruff at the back of your kitten or cat's neck, which is the area of skin that the mother cat uses to pick up and carry her kittens. This is a relatively pain-free procedure.

Kittens are usually vaccinated between eight and nine weeks of age.

Vaccinations given after the primary course are top-ups called 'boosters', which usually only consist of one injection (rather than a course of two). The first booster vaccination is usually given twelve months after the primary vaccination, to ensure a good level of continuing immunity. After this, however, the frequency of further boosters is typically every one to three years depending on the vaccine and the disease risk for your individual cat. Your vet will be able to advise you on how often your cat needs a booster.

Be aware that boarding catteries often require that your cat is fully vaccinated and will need a certificate from your vet to this effect.

Are there any side effects to vaccination?

Adverse effects from vaccinations are rare. The most common side effects are mild, non-specific symptoms of tiredness for twenty-four hours after vaccination and sometimes tenderness and swelling at the injection site. This localized swelling can, in very rare instances (said to be around 1 in 20,000 vaccines), cause a type of malignant tumour (a fibrosarcoma) to develop at the injection site. This is why it is important that you have your cat checked over by the vet straight away if she does develop any swelling after a vaccination.

Due to the very rare nature of these immediate side effects, the main concerns related to vaccination are to do with over-vaccinating – in other words, giving your cat too many boosters. There is a worry that repeated vaccination is linked to chronic disease. Revaccinating a cat that is already protected by a previous booster stimulates their immune system unnecessarily, does nothing to improve their resistance to the disease and may increase the risk of adverse reaction. It is due to these concerns that many vaccine manufacturers have extended their recommended revaccinating interval. One way to help you to assess whether your cat needs their immunity boosting is by having a titre test done (*see* box).

TITRE TESTS

A titre test is a blood test that measures how much immunity an individual has to a particular disease. It checks the level of antibodies in your cat's system. Antibodies are the white blood cells that are important in the immune response, and measuring them helps your vet to know whether your cat needs revaccinating or not. However, antibodies are only one component of your cat's immune system, and there are many other, less easily measurable, ways in which her body protects itself. Therefore titre test results are not an all-encompassing measure of immunity. Another problem is that if the titre test result shows that your cat requires a booster for one particular disease component only, this may not be possible in practice because most vaccines currently come as part and parcel of a multi-agent product.

MATERNAL ANTIBODIES

Kittens acquire some immunity to disease through the protective antibodies in the milk that they suckle from their mother soon after birth. These 'maternal antibodies' provide them with protection during the first six to ten weeks of life. However, after this time they are at risk of infection, which is why you need to start their course of kitten vaccinations around this time. The first vaccine is usually given at around eight or nine weeks of age.

Homeopathic alternatives

It is very unfortunate and misleading that homeopathic remedies called 'nosodes', which are made from the infectious agents we vaccinate cats against, are often termed 'homeopathic vaccinations' because they are not the same as vaccines at all. Homeopathic nosodes are sometimes given in lieu of vaccinations

Homeopathic remedies are not a substitute for vaccination.

because they are believed to offer protection against the infectious diseases without causing any of the adverse reactions associated with conventional vaccines. However, there is no reliable evidence to suggest that they offer any protective immunity to your cat at all. Homeopathic nosodes are certainly not a substitute for vaccinations, and homeopathic veterinary surgeons do not support or recommend using them as such.

The holistic approach to vaccination
It is always important to weigh up all the risks and benefits of any treatment or procedure for your cat, and vaccinations are no different. But, despite concerns, it is important to remember that vaccination offers the most effective way of prevent-

ing your cat from getting a serious infectious disease and that in the vast majority of cases the benefits far outweigh any potential negative effects.

The clearest and most sensible solution is to follow the current World Small Animal Veterinary Association (WSAVA) guidelines. These are based on current scientific knowledge, and recommend that all kittens should receive an initial primary vaccination with a booster twelve months later and then triennially. Core vaccinations should cover feline panleukopenia, feline herpesvirus and calicivirus, and in many cases also feline leukaemia virus. This protocol ensures that your cat receives the best protection against potentially life-threatening diseases, but minimizes the risk of chronic disease through over-vaccination.

Nowadays vets are moving away from the 'one size fits all' approach to vaccination, looking instead at your cat's individual circumstances and needs and tailoring their advice accordingly. Always discuss vaccinations with your vet, to help you evaluate the risk/benefit ratio for your cat and work out the best vaccination protocol for her individual needs.

Remember that vaccination does not always result in 100 per cent protection from disease and is best used as part of an integrated approach to health for your cat.

WORMING

Worming is another important preventive health-care measure for your cat. Cats can harbour various kinds of worms, with roundworms and tapeworms being the most common. All cats are exposed to worm infestation at birth, and are constantly reinfected throughout their lives via ingesting worm eggs in the environment, through grooming or in their prey. Mostly worms do not cause any noticeable effect on your cat's health. However, in significant numbers they can cause your cat to lose weight and body condition, and sometimes also result in diarrhoea, vomiting or irritation around the anus. Worms are also a potential cause of serious diseases in people (*see* box).

Roundworms: these are the most common intestinal worm in cats and occur in kittens and adults alike. The two types of roundworm that cats can harbour are called *Toxocara cati* and *Toxascaris leonina*. Eggs from these worms are passed in the faeces of infected cats and can remain viable in the environment for years. These eggs can then infect other cats or other animals, including mice and other rodents, and then indirectly reinfect cats when they eat their prey. *Toxocara cati* can also be passed from a mother cat to her offspring through her milk. This is why regular treatment for roundworms is important in kittens.

Tapeworm: these are long, flat worms composed of many segments. These can look like grains of rice as they are passed in your cat's faeces. Two types of tapeworm can infect cats: *Dipylidium caninum*, which is usually picked up when a cat ingests infected fleas during grooming, and *Taenia taeniaeformis*, which can be transmitted to the cat when they consume prey such as mice and other rodents. This is the reason why worming is especially important for cats that hunt, and is also why worming treatment goes hand-in-hand with good flea control. In other words, you need to treat your cat for fleas regularly in order to also help prevent her suffering from tapeworm infection.

TOXOPLASMOSIS

This is a disease caused by infection with a single-celled parasitic organism called *Toxoplasma gondii*. It is the most publicized disease that humans can get from cats. It is, however, extremely rare that infection with this parasite is due to contact with cats, and it is much more likely to be acquired through eating undercooked meat. Infection is generally only a problem in immuno-compromised people and pregnant women (where it can harm the developing foetus). Control measures are especially important in these groups of people; it is recommended that they should not handle cat litter and should pay close attention to hygiene after handling cats (as well as cooking meat properly, of course).

Treatment

Regular treatment for worms is recommended, since most cats harbour them without showing any obvious signs. Every three to six months is considered enough for most adult cats, though it may be more frequent depending on certain risk factors. For example, worming may be required more frequently if your cat is a prolific hunter and hence may be exposed to picking up tapeworms from the mice and rodents she catches. Kittens need more frequent worming because they can harbour roundworms passed on to them from their mother. Your vet will weigh and worm your kitten when you take her in for her primary course of vaccines. Kittens are usually wormed every fortnight from three to eight weeks old, and then monthly until they are six months old. From then on follow the recommendations for adult cats.

There are many different worming products on the market and they vary in terms of ease of administration as well as efficacy.

Whilst most current worming products available for cats are considered safe, not all of them are equally effective and some work against certain types of worm and not others. This is why it is best to ask your vet's advice about the most appropriate and effective product for your cat. They will advise you as to the safest and most effective treatment for your individual cat's needs, based on her age and life-style, and how easy she is to tablet! The vet will also weigh your cat and ensure that she gets the correct dose of worm-er. Worming treatments come in a wide range of different formulations, includ-ing injectable as well as liquid 'spot-on' form, so that even cats that spit out tab-lets can be wormed!

Finally, do not forget that flea control is an important part of worm control, because fleas can transmit a type of tape-worm (*Dipylidium caninum*) to your cat.

Other control measures

It is important to use worming products judiciously because, as with the too-fre-quent use of any medicines, resistance can build up in the worms that we are trying to eradicate. This has already happened with horses and farm animals where resistance to commonly used worming products is a big problem.

A more targeted approach to worming, and a good way of reducing unnecessary treatment, is to take a faecal sample to your vet. A test called a faecal egg count will alert you as to whether it is necessary to worm your cat.

Natural methods

It is widely accepted that natural reme-dies are not usually an effective method of worm control. While some of these measures may help to reduce a worm burden, they are generally not enough on their own. Indeed, some over-the-coun-ter herbal wormers are excessively harsh

Worming is usually important for all cats.

RINGWORM

Ringworm is a fungal infection that can affect cats as well as people. Your cat can catch ringworm from the environment and then pass it on to you, sometimes without showing any symptoms herself. If your cat has ringworm, wear gloves when you handle her and do not allow children and other susceptible individuals to come into contact with her. If you do have ringworm, then it is safe to assume that your cat is a carrier and you will need to treat your home and your cat as well as yourself, following your doctor's as well as your vet's advice. If your cat does show symptoms, then these include hair loss in a circular pattern and she may or may not be itchy.

FLEAS

The most common flea found on cats is the cat flea, *Ctenocephalides felis* (which is also the most common type found on dogs). Fleas live by biting your cat and injecting anticoagulants into her system and then feeding on her blood. Most cats harbour a few fleas at some stage in their lives and show no more adverse effects than mild irritation and scratching.

However, severe flea infestations can be a real problem, and can even cause anaemia in very young kittens. Fleas can also carry the larval stage of tapeworms, infecting your cat as they groom themselves. In addition, fleas can affect people, causing irritating bites to areas such as the ankles.

Flea treatment is also especially crucial in cats that suffer from an allergy to fleas. In such cases, a single bite can trigger a cycle of itching and scratching that will cause great discomfort to the cat and can result in serious skin disease.

on your cat's system and can cause nasty reactions. Moreover, there are no homeopathic remedies for worming, because homeopathy works by treating the individual rather than the disease. Therefore, all in all, due to the potentially toxic and variably effective nature of some 'natural' worming measures, it is usually far safer and more effective to use conventional worming treatments, taking care to use them judiciously.

Finally, because it was recognized that worms are greatly influenced by the moon, worming of animals was traditionally done at certain times of the month. Worms are known to be more active when the moon is waxing, and so will be less well buried in the host's tissues at this time, and thus easier to get rid of.

HOW TO TEST FOR FLEAS

You may spot fleas if you go through your cat's coat carefully; they are 2mm-long red-brown, wingless insects. Another way of checking for fleas is to moisten a piece of white paper and place it beneath your cat, and then brush her so that dander falls on the paper. If you see little black specs that turn a red-brown, then that is positive for fleas, as this occurs when flea droppings, containing blood, dissolve in the moisture. However, a negative test cannot rule out fleas.

This is why flea prevention and treatment are an important part of your cat's routine preventive health care.

The flea lifecycle

The entire flea lifecycle, from egg to adult, takes anything between two weeks and eight months. Adult fleas spend most of their time on your cat, where the females lay eggs that then contaminate the home environment. Once in the carpet and your home's soft furnishings, the eggs develop into larvae, which then form pupae; in the right conditions, these develop into adults which jump back onto your cat.

Fleas thrive in warm, humid conditions, and do less well in extremes of temperature and in the dry. This is why, although they can be a problem all year round, fleas are usually more of an issue in the spring and autumn when the conditions are most favourable for them. In addition, fleas can stay dormant in the environment for many months, waiting for ambient conditions that will allow them to re-emerge. So if you move into a new home where the previous residents had pets, be extra vigilant in cleaning before you introduce your cat.

Effective flea control requires a two-pronged attack: killing adult fleas on your cat (and any other pets), and helping to prevent reinfestation from the environment by treating the house.

Treatment

Flea treatments for your cat come in various different forms; currently the most popular treatments are 'spot-ons'. These are pipettes filled with an insecticide liquid that is poured onto the back of your cat's neck, between her shoulder blades, usually once a month. This is then absorbed into her skin and sebaceous glands and is thus spread throughout the

> **READ LABELS VERY CAREFULLY**
>
> Be very careful when you use spot-on products and never use a flea product on a cat that has been formulated for use on a dog. This is because some dog products contain permethrin, or a related compound, that can be lethal to cats. Keep a recently treated dog well away from contact with your cat, as even mild exposure can be toxic.

whole body, killing any fleas as soon as they bite her. Some preparations do not only kill the flea itself, but also act to disrupt its breeding and lifecycle, hence are a more effective way of preventing reinfestation. It is a good idea to wear gloves when you are handling these spot-ons, and not to touch the treated skin for several hours afterwards.

Flea collars, powders, sprays and tablets are other methods of flea control for your cat, and are of varying efficacy depending on their active constituents. Be especially wary of flea collars, as in general these are not very effective treatments,

Some cats are highly sensitive to fleas.

may cause localized skin irritation and can also be dangerous unless they have a quick release safety catch.

The most common reasons for flea treatments not working are if they contain ineffective ingredients, are incorrectly applied or administered, or if not all pets in the household are treated. Your vet will be able to advise on a suitable treatment for your cat and show you how to use it.

Environmental control measures

Since most stages of the flea's lifecycle take place in the environment, treating your cat is just one part of an overall strategy of flea control. Some 90 per cent of the flea's lifecycle – the egg, pupae and larval stages – takes place away from your cat, so it is easy to see why environmental measures are the mainstay of effective flea control. These immature stages of the flea will be present in your cat's home environment, in her bedding, on your carpets and soft furnishings and in any nooks and crannies where the conditions are right for them.

The simplest means of getting rid of flea larvae, pupae and eggs from your home is to vacuum regularly and wash your cat's bedding every few weeks on a hot cycle. If you have carpets then steam cleaning them is also recommended. Bear in mind that wooden and laminate floors are much less flea-friendly environments. There are also various household sprays that have active ingredients to control the flea lifecycle.

Finally, do not forget that every time your cat comes into contact with other cats, or with dogs, she can potentially pick up a new crop of fleas. She can then bring them back into the house, and so start the whole flea cycle off all over again. This is why flea prevention is an ongoing process.

Natural methods

As with internal parasites, a few fleas are to be expected, as your cat can pick them up whenever she goes out or meets another cat or catches a rodent, for example, even if your home is flea-free. For most cats, feeding them well and thereby ensuring that they have a robust immune system and a shiny coat rich in natural oils will help to prevent them being unduly affected by fleas. In addition to these overall health and dietary means, using natural methods of flea prevention, such as regular flea combing and the use of safe and natural repellents, alongside rigorous vacuuming, should be enough in most cases.

Many natural products have been put forward over the years as having flea-killing or flea-repellent properties. These include concentrated eucalyptus oil, pennyroyal oil, tea tree oil, neem oil, citrus oil and D-limonene. Whilst some of these constituents are found in effective, licensed products, many are actually potentially toxic for cats and are also not effective. If you have any doubts about a natural or alternative method of flea prevention, always ask your vet first before using it

---

ALTERNATIVE FLEA PRODUCTS

Garlic, yeast and vitamin B have all been touted as having anti-flea properties, but scientific studies have not demonstrated that they work, and indeed they can be toxic to cats. Similarly, the use of desiccants, borax or diatomaceous earth, is sometimes advocated to help control fleas in the home, but these should also be avoided as they can be toxic to cats if inhaled or ingested.

CAT BITES AND SCRATCHES

A word of caution about cat bites and scratches – one potential side effect of your attempts to worm or apply flea treatment to your feline friend! Cat scratches can sometimes transmit bacteria called *Bartonella henselae*, which can cause a fever-type illness commonly called 'cat scratch fever' in people. Children and people with an impaired immune system are particularly at risk. Similarly, cat bites can cause painful, swollen reactions and abscesses because a cat's mouth (and claws) contain a multitude of bacteria. Always wash wounds thoroughly with anti-bacterial soap and seek medical attention if you are bitten or scratched by a cat.

on your cat. One non-toxic weapon in the war on fleas is to simply use a flea comb on your cat regularly. These have tines that are so fine that they will mechanically rid your cat's coat of the fleas quickly and efficiently.

However, if fleas are still a problem, or if your cat has a particular sensitivity to them, then the judicious use of insecticide spot-ons is justified. This helps to break the flea lifecycle and enables you to get on top of the situation before a few fleas rapidly become a lot of fleas. But it is as well to try to use these insecticides as little as possible, because as well as being harsh for your cat's system, the chemicals in most flea treatments will eventually end up reaching waterways and landfill sites, and thus can affect the environment. Indeed, the class of insecticides widely blamed for the recent mass

disappearance of the honeybee is in fact closely related to the active constituent in the most commonly used spot-on flea treatments. If these products can harm fleas and bees, perhaps we should be concerned about the possible long-term consequences of monthly applications to your cat.

NEUTERING

Neutering is the general term used to describe 'de-sexing' an animal; it means the same as spaying in females and castrating in males.

Spaying is usually an operation to remove the entire female reproductive tract, similar to an ovariohysterectomy in women. (However, there are new methods where only the cat's ovaries are removed). Spay surgery is commonly performed through the cat's flank area or their tummy, and the fur in either of these areas will be clipped away for the operation. (Be aware that the fur may grow back a slightly different colour, so if you have a show cat, for instance, discuss

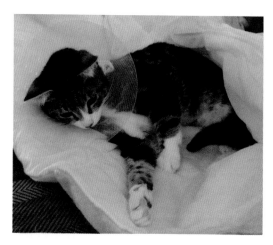

Female cats may need to wear a buster collar after they have been spayed.

Choose a cat-friendly practice.

CHOOSING A CAT-FRIENDLY VETERINARY PRACTICE

You may be lucky enough to be able to register your cat at a practice that is cat only, or one that is especially cat-friendly and runs cat-only clinics at certain times of day. These measures avoid the added stress of barking dogs upsetting your cat in the waiting room, and should also mean that the vets and practice staff are especially amenable to looking after feline patients. When choosing a veterinary practice for your cat, always visit the clinic first to make sure that you are happy that the staff are friendly, helpful and knowledge-able and that the premises are clean and cat-friendly. Most practices offer a free initial check-up consultation for new clients and will be amenable to showing you around the place (as long as they are not too busy).

this with your vet before the operation.) Castration is the removal of the testes.

Both operations are performed under general anaesthesia and, although they are major operations, they are procedures that your vet will be doing every day. In most cases your cat will only be kept in the veterinary hospital for the day, being released to go home in the evening. They will have to return to the surgery for post-operative checks and sometimes for the removal of stitches (in females only, as castration doesn't usually involve any skin stitches). You should keep your cat quiet for a few weeks following the surgery; this is especially important for females, as their operation was bigger.

Some practices have a special area of the waiting room for cats only.

The benefits of neutering

There are many benefits to neutering both male and female cats. Most simply, these add up to the fact that it is a safe and effective way of helping to maintain your cat's health and longevity and to help prevent adding to the unwanted or stray cat population. In addition, the list of antisocial habits of the unneutered cat, such as the loud and incessant 'calling' of the female and unpleasant scent marking and spraying in the male, make it a fairly sensible and straightforward decision for most owners to take.

As well as preventing unwanted pregnancies, the benefits of neutering female cats include a lower risk of mammary cancer and pyometra (a serious infection in the womb). Having your female cat neutered will also prevent such nuisance behaviours as the aforementioned 'calling', where they cry loudly and incessantly and can become restless and agitated. Unneutered females will do this every few weeks from February through to the autumn, if they do not get pregnant. It is an indication that they are 'in season' and sexually receptive. They are calling for male cats, which will then arrive on your doorstep bringing with them such antisocial activities as fighting, spraying and caterwauling!

The benefits of having a male cat neutered are equally important. Castrated males have a much lower tendency to get into fights with other cats and so have a much reduced risk of contracting life-threatening viral diseases such as feline immunodeficiency virus (FIV) and feline leukaemia virus (FeLV). They will also have fewer problems associated with cat bite abscesses and other injuries sustained through fighting. In addition, because they tend to wander over a larger distance, entire tomcats may also be at greater risk from road traffic accidents. Finally, not many people can cope with living with entire toms because of their pungent, territorial scent marking (including around the house) and the fact that they are often less easy to handle.

The optimum age to neuter

This has traditionally been at around six months of age for both female and male cats as this is the age at which they usually reach sexual maturity and can potentially begin to reproduce. However, more recently there has been a drive towards neutering cats earlier, at between four and five months of age. This earlier neutering has not been shown to cause any detrimental effects in terms of development or growth and is increasingly common. Always have a chat with your vet to determine the best age for your individual youngster to be neutered, as the age of sexual maturity can vary with the breed of cat and the most practical time to neuter can depend on your circumstances.

Some owners have their kittens neutered before they allow them outside for the first time, and will also have them

---

NEUTERING AND OBESITY

The metabolic rate of neutered animals is usually around 20 per cent lower than that of their entire counterparts and neutered animals tend to have a keener interest in food. Both of these facts can lead to cats of either sex gaining weight after neutering. However, this situation can be avoided by altering your cat's diet to match their lower energy requirements, and of course by simply not over-feeding them (*see* Chapter 7).

microchipped whilst they are under anaesthetic. In these instances, earlier neutering can be advantageous because it will mean that your kitten can go outside at an earlier stage and have fewer frustrating weeks spent indoors.

SUPPLEMENTS FOR CATS

In this second part of the chapter we are taking an in-depth look at some of the most widely used supplements for cats, so that you can choose one that is both appropriate and effective whatever your cat's age or ailment.

Supplements are used to promote health and prevent disease. In simple terms these are products derived from natural substances that have been refined, concentrated and sometimes adapted to provide a specific health-giving effect. They are usually given to your cat daily, with food, in the form of powders, tablets, capsules or liquids, and are recommended for problems such as arthritis, skin disease and for promoting overall health. Examples of commonly used supplements include glucosamines, essential fatty acids and certain minerals and vitamins.

'Nutraceuticals' was coined as a marketing term to make supplements sound more akin to 'pharmaceuticals', and hence more effective. Whilst it is excellent news that there are so many cat-friendly health products out there, they can vary widely in terms of quality and effectiveness, which can sometimes make choosing the right one difficult.

Supplements are used to promote health.

Does your cat need a supplement?

Healthy cats should not, in theory, require any supplements. However, we live in a less than perfect world. In reality, our cats are not always getting a diet of a wide range of freshly prepared, 100 per cent organic meat, colourful vegetables and fruits in a completely stress-free environment. Commonly, a lot of the nutritional value of food is lost through intensive farming, processing and cooking. This is especially the case for cats fed on commercially prepared, mass-produced foods such as canned meat and biscuits. Added to this, remember that manufacturers attempt to balance the nutrients in their diets based on guidelines for an average cat. But as each cat is an individual and will differ in how well they digest and utilize their food, not all of them will thrive on these diets. This is how the need for supplements arises.

Another situation where the use of supplements may be warranted is if your cat is unwell, and hence has an increased need for particular building blocks to help her body repair and heal. Older cats too are prime candidates for dietary supplements, to help support the degenerative changes relating to old age.

How to choose a supplement

With so many different supplements now available for cats, and with a great deal of variation between them in terms of quality, cost and effectiveness, you can (and should) be fussy. And do not be afraid to contact the manufacturers directly if you need more information on their products.

The following are the key guidelines for helping you select high-quality supplements. Focus on purity, quality and quantity, and you won't go far wrong.

How much active ingredient does it contain and what is its purity? This can vary widely, from high-quality, human-grade ingredients to those with hardly any active constituent in them at all. Also appreciate that the active component needs to be in a form that your cat can utilize, in order to be effective (*see* Bioavailability).

What other ingredients does it contain? All ingredients should be listed on the label. If you are unsure, ask the manufacturer what the purpose of each ingredient is and why it is included.

Where is it sourced? Find out where the product comes from and how it is manufactured, so that you can be sure that it is ethically and sustainably produced. This is especially important for supplements such as chondroitin (which can potentially come from shark cartilage), and for any fish supplement, making sure it is not from wild-caught stock.

Will using an equivalent human supplement be just as good? For example, if both of you take glucosamine for your aching joints, or an antioxidant to support your immune system, can you give your supplement to your cat? In most cases your cat's supplement will have been specifically formulated to be more effective and palatable for her. Always pay attention to the quality and quantity of the active ingredient, and buy the best and most appropriate one for your cat that you can.

What is the dose and what is the cost per day? Do check this, because it can be misleading. Work out how much of the supplement your cat will need per day, and hence what it will cost on a daily basis. This will allow you to compare prices. Cheaper compounds are less likely to offer high quality; you usually do get what you pay for.

What formulation is it and will your cat take it? This is of crucial importance! Only you know how fussy and wriggly your cat can be and how tricky it may be to get her to take the supplement. Sometimes it is easier to get a liquid formulation for those cats that are difficult with tablets, or you might consider capsules that can be opened and sprinkled onto the food.

Check it has a batch number and expiry date. This is a legal requirement.

What are the health claims and is there any data or research to back these up? Supplement manufacturers are not allowed to make any specific claims that their products can be used to 'treat', let alone 'cure', a named condition. There are strict guidelines that only allow the use of broad phrases, such as 'promote' or 'improve' health.

Make yourself aware of any potential side effects: Usually supplements are relatively safe to use. However, there can be side effects and supplements can also contain contaminants that can also cause problems. This is why the use of any supplements needs to be under the guidance of your vet.

Instructions for use. The label should give recommendations for daily amounts, including information on how the supplement needs to be stored.

Echinacea is a herbal remedy often used to boost the immune system.

BIOAVAILABILITY

Bioavailability is a measure of how effectively a supplement can be used by the body. For instance, it may be the highest-quality, most expensive supplement, but if it is parcelled up into a capsule, or chemically bonded to another constituent that makes it difficult for the body to use, then it is effectively useless. High bioavailability means that the active constituent of the supplement will be able to be used to maximum effect by your cat. Of course bioavailability is something that the manufacturer of the supplement should be aware of, but it is still a factor that you should check when selecting a supplement.

Scientific evidence. Some companies have begun providing data for their products through independent scientific studies, but be aware that testimonials are not the same as evidence or proof of efficacy – they are simply someone's opinion.

General guidelines for the use of supplements

Supplements, unlike most medications, work slowly and it is likely to take several weeks before you start to notice any benefits. It is also a good idea to introduce them slowly: start by giving your cat around half the recommended dose for a few weeks, before building up to the full amount. This enables her body to get used it, and in the rare instances where there are any sensitivities, these can be addressed. The exception to this is glucosamine supplements. These are usually given at a double dose to begin with, and then reduced down to a maintenance level after a number of weeks (but always follow the directions given on the label).

Remember that supplements need to be used appropriately and carefully and that they are never a substitute for a good diet or normal veterinary care. Do check with your vet before you start your cat on any supplement, to make sure that it is suitable for her, and also let your vet know if your cat has a reaction to them.

A ROUGH GUIDE TO COMMONLY USED SUPPLEMENTS

Antioxidants

Antioxidants are substances that help to protect the body from the damaging effects of free radicals. Free radicals are highly reactive molecules that are made in the body all the time; they are a natural waste product of many everyday processes. However, stress and exposure to toxins in food and the environment causes an increased production. Free radicals damage cells and are involved in many chronic, degenerative conditions.

Antioxidants are the body's natural

Milk thistle is an important antioxidant.

defence against free radicals and are provided, in part, by the array of fresh foods in the diet and include vitamins A, C and E as well as selenium and alpha-linolenic acid. They play a key role in maintaining health and preventing disease.

What are they used for?
Most cats will be exposed to the factors that cause increased free radical production on a daily basis, from the pollution in the air they breathe to the pesticide residues in the foods they eat. Therefore antioxidants are a valuable supplement for a lot of cats. However, they may be particularly beneficial for elderly cats and for those suffering from any degenerative conditions. They can also play a role in supporting cats suffering from immune-mediated diseases, as well as cancer. Antioxidants can also help to promote recovery after serious illness, and are often given to cats which are on ongoing medications.

Essential fatty acids

Essential fatty acids (EFAs) are essential components of your cat's daily diet and are termed essential because they cannot be manufactured by the body and must come from the diet. EFAs are crucial to every cell in the body, and aid in the regulation of nearly every bodily function, including helping to maintain a healthy skin and coat and a strong immune system. Cats in particular have an absolute need for a certain essential fatty acid called arachidonic acid, as unlike dogs, they have only a limited ability to manufacture this from other fatty acids. Arachidonic acid is found in animal fats, so this is another reason for your cat needing a carnivorous, meaty diet.

Essential fatty acids have two main families: omega-3s and omega-6s. These come from different sources and their primary action in the body is also slightly different. The omega-3s – eicosapentae-noic acid (EPA) and docosahexaenoic acid (DHA) – are principally found in fish oils and these make excellent supplements for cats. Especially rich sources are deep sea cold-water fish such as salmon, mackerel, halibut and herring. Flax seed oil is one of the richest plant sources of the omega-3 oil alpha-linolenic acid (ALA). However, cats have a limited ability to process seed sources of omega-3s effectively, so your cat is far better off having a fish-based omega-3 supplement. Omega-3s can be described as having a generally anti-inflammatory action in the body and are recommended in maintaining skin and coat health, as well as for kidney, brain and joint function.

The omega-6s, on the other hand – gamma linolenic acid (GLA) and linoleic acid (LA) – are readily derived from most vegetable and plant oils, as well as some meat and dairy products. Borage is a very good source of omega-6, and much more concentrated than evening primrose oil. These are primarily indicated for skin and coat health.

If your cat is receiving any EFA supplement (whether it is omega-3 or omega-6), make sure that she is also getting enough vitamin E in her diet, either within the EFA supplement or separately.

What are they used for?
A balanced omega-3/omega-6 supplement is often recommended for promoting a healthy skin and coat and may be indicated for cats that suffer from skin allergies as they can help to reduce itching and improve dry, flaky skin. Choose a supplement that is specifically rich in omega-3 for cats with heart conditions, cognitive dysfunction and for those with kidney disease.

Use of glucosamine and related products
Glucosamines are complex sugar-type molecules that are produced naturally in the body. They are used for the repair of connective tissues, such as cartilage, by stimulating the production of gly-cosaminoglycans (GAGs). Glucosamines can be refined from natural sources, usually from shellfish, and given as supplements to augment the body's own production. This is especially necessary when demand exceeds the body's normal production, such as in old age and arthritis.

There is significant evidence to support their efficacy, and they are widely used in the management of degenerative joint disease. However, these supplements do much more than help repair and rebuild cartilage; they actually act to slow down its destruction. In addition, glucosamine has also been shown to have an anti-inflammatory action, helping to relieve some of the joint pain in arthritis.

As well as being used on its own, glucosamine is commonly combined with other active constituents such as chondroitin sulfate or methylsulfonylmethane (MSM) for suggested further benefits. The green-lipped mussel (*Perna canaliculus*) is cultivated exclusively in the pure coastal waters around New Zealand, and is an excellent and unique natural source of glucosamine and chondroitin.

9 HOLISTIC TREATMENTS FOR COMMON AILMENTS

This chapter will give an overview of the main complementary treatments used for common ailments in cats. There are whole books dedicated to this topic, but the aim in this chapter is merely to illustrate how complementary medicine can form part of an integrated approach to treatment for your cat. Some of the suggested treatments you will be able to do at home, but others need specialist care. Preventive health care and holistic management methods are also outlined.

For details on how to use some of the treatments outlined, such as dosage and use of herbal or homeopathic remedies, please refer to Chapter 1. Holistic treatments for common ailments in kittens and elderly cats are given at the end of Chapters 4 and 5, respectively. Always seek professional advice before using any form of complementary medicine to treat

your cat, as dosage can vary and some herbal remedies, for instance, are not suitable for every patient and can even be toxic if used inappropriately. Always let your vet know if you are using any form of complementary treatment for your cat, especially if she is on any ongoing medications.

Note: if your cat is unwell in any way then she should be taken to the vet for diagnosis and treatment. The advice given here in no way replaces that of your veterinary surgeon for any ill animal.

SKIN AND COAT

It is well known that a shiny, glossy coat is an indicator of good health in an animal, just as a dull coat is often an indication that they may be unwell. This is linked to the fact that as well as its role in protection and sensation, the skin is one of the body's key detoxification organs. Nowhere else does your cat's diet and nutritional status reflect itself more clearly than in the state of her skin and coat. Persistent or severe skin and coat complaints need to be checked by your vet so that they can diagnose the cause of the problem and advise the correct treatment.

Other than vaccinations, skin problems are the number one reason why cats are taken to the vets. Itching, which in veterinary terms is called pruritus, is the most common symptom of a skin prob-

Calendula officinalis *is a herbal remedy with healing and antiseptic actions.*

lem. Your cat may scratch, itch, bite and lick herself all over, or may concentrate on certain parts of her body. Dry skin and dandruff can be other common skin complaints that affect your cat, as can an excessively greasy or oily coat. Your cat may lose her fur and develop bald areas or red and sore patches due to excessive and persistent licking, scratching or rubbing at them.

Routine care for a healthy skin and coat
Essential fatty acids are the most important supplement for maintaining a healthy, shiny and itch-free skin and coat. These are the building blocks of the skin, and also have anti-inflammatory action to relieve itching. They are a must-have for any cat with a skin condition such as an allergy. Give a balanced supplement of omega-6 and omega-3, found in evening primrose and fish oils, or, to make it easier, choose a good-quality proprietary supplement, which should also contain vitamin E.

It is important to keep on top of flea control measures for all cats (*see* Chapter 8), but especially for those with flea allergies, where it only takes one fleabite to trigger a reaction.

Brushing your cat every day is an important part of her routine health care, especially for long-haired individuals, because as well as keeping them tangle-free, it stimulates the skin's oil-producing glands, helping to keep their coats waterproof.

Common problems of the skin and coat
Miliary dermatitis and allergies
This is probably the most common ongoing skin complaint in cats. Miliary dermatitis is a condition where scabs develop on a cat's skin, especially along their back and at the base of their tail, and their coat becomes greasy or dry and flaky. Cats

Cats with allergies tend to groom themselves constantly.

with this complaint will groom themselves constantly and bite and lick at their skin, making it sore, and will have a thinning coat. The most common cause of miliary dermatitis is an allergy to fleas.

Allergies are an exaggerated and unnecessary response of the immune system to a harmless substance, known as an allergen. According to holistic thinking, allergies are caused by an unbalanced immune system that is over-reactive and develops an allergy to whatever potential allergens are around. Thus fleas do not cause a flea allergy; rather the cat is already potentially allergic, and fleas are common in their home environment, so the cat develops an allergy to flea saliva. A single bite from one flea can then trigger flea allergy dermatitis. This means that it becomes crucial to be vigilant about flea control for such cats. You usually have to use more than one method of flea control, such as a 'spot-on' to kill adult fleas as well as a household treatment to take care of the rest of their lifecycle.

If miliary dermatitis continues after fleas have been completely eliminated, then it may be that your cat is suffering from a different allergic skin disease such as a food allergy; however, this is far less common. Your vet will help you to make the correct diagnosis.

Cat bite abscesses

Due to the high bacterial load carried in cats' mouths and claws, cat fight injuries tend to result in abscesses. These are often seen as swellings around the cat's head and neck area (or to their back end, if they were trying to run away!) They can result in your cat running a fever and feeling quite off-colour until the abscess is either lanced by the vet or bursts spontaneously, releasing the pressure and allowing the infection (a thick pus) to drain away.

A visit to the vet is usually important for any cat bite abscess. They will clip and clean the area and assess any complications, such as injuries to the mouth, eyes or ears. It is likely that your cat will benefit from a course of antibiotics to help rid her of the infection quickly and prevent any complications. However, in addition you may also be able to help to clean the wound daily with a hypercal solution (a homeopathic antiseptic tincture), or warm, salty water. Use of the herb cleavers (*Galium aparine*), given as a tea on your cat's food, can also be beneficial to help drain the lymphatic system and clear infection after an abscess.

Ringworm

This is a fungal skin complaint detailed in Chapter 8.

Solar dermatitis and skin tumours

If cats with white, non-pigmented areas of skin are exposed to too much sun they can suffer from serious inflammation at the tips of their ears and on their noses. This can cause sunburn or even skin cancer, so these cats need to have high factor sunblock (SPF 30 or more) applied to these areas in the summer.

Complementary treatments for the skin and coat

Homeopathic remedies: sulphur is the number one homeopathic remedy for skin complaints. It is used for cats with itchy, smelly skin that is hot to the touch. Arsenicum album is indicated if the skin is dry and scaly, with the itching being worse at night, and if the cat is restless. The dose for these remedies is usually one tablet twice a day for up to five days, using a 12c or 30c potency.

Topical treatment for sore or ulcerated areas: clip the fur away from the lesion and then you can bathe it with a solution of hypercal (a homeopathic antiseptic tincture), or warm, salty, sterile (or boiled) water. Soothing aloe vera gel or hypercal cream can then be applied to the area twice daily. An oatmeal compress can also be used; this is soothing and helps to relieve the itch. Alternatively, you can apply a green tea bag to the area as a cold

---

BATHING YOUR CAT

It will come as no surprise to learn that cats hate to be bathed! Luckily there are not many occasions when it is necessary. However, using a soothing, oatmeal-based soak on an itchy cat can be very beneficial. Place a handful of oats inside a sock or stocking and swish around in a little warm water, to leave a milky residue. Then dip a sponge or wet cloth into this milky mixture and apply it to your cat's affected areas. Rinse off after ten minutes.

poultice, as this is full of antioxidants and is astringent so helps to dry the area. Or you could apply an oatmeal soak to help soothe and relieve itching (*see* box).

EARS

Cats with ear complaints can suffer from symptoms that range from the odd shake of their head to persistent ear irritation with vigorous scratching where one or both ears become red and painful. There may even be a smelly, crusty discharge at the opening to the ear, and your cat may also cry if you touch her ears. If she has persistent or severe head shaking, or is holding her head to one side, then this may be a sign of a foreign body such as a grass seed in her ear; this is a particular problem during the spring and summer months.

Recurrent or ongoing ear problems are usually a symptom of a more deep-rooted disease, requiring more in-depth treatment for a lasting cure.

Symptoms of middle and inner ear disease include loss of balance, nausea and disorientation, which are also signs of several other serious illnesses that will equally require rapid veterinary attention.

Due to the wide variety of possible causes, it is important to have any ear condition diagnosed by the vet so that the correct form of treatment can be used.

Routine care for healthy ears

For routine cleaning of healthy ears use a few drops of olive oil (or almond oil) on a piece of cotton wool and gently wipe the outer ear to remove any excess wax. You can equally just use damp cotton wool to gently wipe away any debris or dirt from the outer ear canal. Never use cotton buds as they can damage and irritate the delicate lining of the ear canals.

Common ear problems
Ear mites
These mainly affect kittens, but they can occur in a cat at any age, and are highly contagious to other cats and dogs. They are tiny parasites that can infect the cat's ear canals, causing a lot of irritation as they feed on wax and debris. Cats with ear mites will scratch their ears vigorously and shake their heads, and there will usually be evidence of dark brown or black debris in their ears.

Your vet will be able to diagnose whether your cat is suffering from ear mites by examining the ear canal and sometimes by taking a swab of the waxy debris and identifying the mites under the microscope. The common and straightforward treatment involves regular application of a spot-on flea treatment (applied to the back of the neck) that also kills ear mites, as well as the use of ear drops to medicate the ear and to clean and soothe the ear canals. Successful treatment for ear mites needs to exactly follow your vet's instructions, which will often involve repeating the spot-on or ear drops several weeks later, as this will kill any newly emerging mites that were not targeted the first time.

Complementary treatments for ear complaints
Ear drops: puncture one capsule of vitamin E and mix the contents with two teaspoons of olive oil, and add a drop of grape seed extract. This is a good antiseptic mixture and is effective as an antifungal and anti-bacterial agent, helping to fight ear infections. Apply these drops in the ear twice a day for a week, gently massaging the base of the ear after each application. An alternative is to use a dilute homeopathic hypercal solution to douche the ear; this is more applicable if there is not excessive wax.

Always make sure that your vet has checked your cat's ears first, as you should never put drops into her ears if she is suffering from middle or inner ear disease.

Homeopathic remedies: Belladonna, 30c, for sudden onset conditions where the ears are painful, red and hot. Sulphur, 30c, may be considered if the ear problem is part of a generalized skin complaint, and they are hot. Both can be used twice daily for seven days.

Remedy for swollen ear flaps: your cat can suffer from swelling to one of her ear flaps (aural haematomas). This happens when the small capillaries in the ear break as your cat shakes her head vigorously, and is usually due to an underlying ear infection. The homeopathic remedy arnica, used at a 30c potency twice daily for five days, can be used to help with the bleeding and bruising of this condition. This can be given in conjunction with draining and/or the use of ear drops for any underlying infection.

EYES

Eyes are complicated structures, and problems can affect any part of them from the lids, to the clear surface of the eye (the cornea), to the lens or the glands that produce the lubricating tears. Discharge from the corners of one or both eyes is a common symptom of an eye problem in cats. This is usually green or yellow and may affect one or both eyes, or go from one to the other. Your cat may also have her third eyelid (the protective membrane that comes across her eye to protect it) drawn across her eye when there is a problem. Cloudiness, excessive discharge and even watery discharge can also spell problems. Similarly, if your cat is squinting or seems uncomfortable

in bright light, these are symptoms of a potentially serious eye complaint.

It always pays to have any problem with your cat's eyes seen to by your vet as soon as possible because seemingly minor symptoms can actually require urgent veterinary treatment in order to save your cat's eyesight. Your vet should examine any eye condition, however mild, straight away.

Routine care for healthy eyes

Make sure that your cat does not have to endure long-term exposure to a smoky environment or air pollution. It is also a good idea not to use air fresheners or other household sprays near your cat, as these can be irritating.

Always check with the vet before using any topical eyewash on your cat.

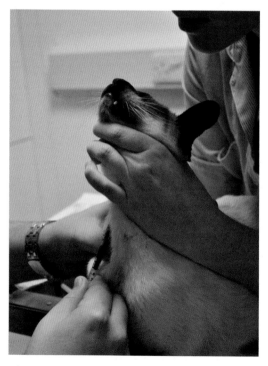

This cat is having a blood sample taken.

Common eye complaints
Conjunctivitis
This is a common eye complaint where the mucus membranes surrounding the eye (the conjunctiva) are red, sore and swollen. There is also usually a discharge from the inner corners of the eyes which can be a thick yellow or green colour or watery. Viruses or bacteria, or commonly both, can cause conjunctivitis. One of the principal viruses involved in conjunctivitis is the herpesvirus, and other pathogens involved in 'cat flu' such as calicivirus and chlamydophila. Hence cats with conjunctivitis may also have other symptoms of cat flu, such as sneezing and nasal discharge. Conjunctivitis can also be linked to problems caused by the anatomy of your cat's face, for example in the flat face of Persians, causing the tear ducts to become squashed and hence prone to blockage and infection.

Depending on the cause, conjunctivitis is usually treated with antibiotics and eye drops.

Corneal ulcers
These are scratches on the cornea – the clear surface of the eye. Cats commonly get corneal ulcers due to a scratch from another cat or via a bramble or other trauma. They can also occur due to dryness of the eye itself, making it more prone to injury, due to a lack of normal tear production or inadequate eyelid function. Again, this can be connected with certain breeds of cat that have protruding eyes so that their eyelids may not meet fully over the globe and thus cannot ensure that the tears cleanse the eye properly. Cats with corneal ulcers may also have accompanying conjunctivitis.

Treatment usually involves eye drops and sometimes tablets or other medications too. It is important to get corneal ulcers treated promptly, as they can be very painful.

Complementary treatments for eye complaints
Eye drops: a basic eyewash can be made by adding one or two drops of the homeopathic tincture euphrasia to sterile saline eye-irrigating solution. Bathe the eye twice or three times daily for up to a week.

Herbal remedies: the herb eyebright is supportive for any eye complaint.

Homeopathic remedies: euphrasia eye drops can be used to support the majority of eye complaints. The following remedies are indicated for conjunctivitis: Allium cepa, where the conjunctiva is red and inflamed, and the discharge profuse and watery; and pulsatilla, if the discharge is bland and creamy, and the conjunctivitis alternates from one eye to the other. Sulphur is the remedy of choice for sore, dry eyes where the eyelids are red. These remedies are usually used at a 12c or 30c potency twice daily for a week.

TEETH AND GUMS

Diet plays a major role in your cat's dental health. Cats that are fed solely on commercial wet diets are at great risk of developing gum disease than those where some dry foods, or raw meaty bones, are also offered. This is because diets that encourage chewing are more effective than sticky, soft diets at preventing the accumulation of plaque and subsequently tartar on the surface of the teeth, and hence the development of gum disease (gingivitis). Chewing also stimulates saliva production, which helps keep the mouth healthy and clean.

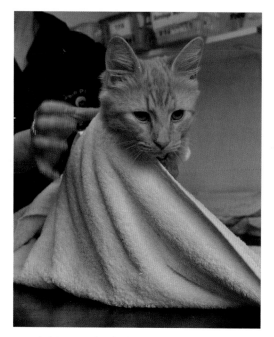

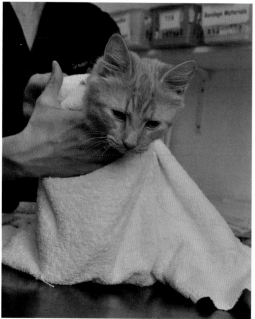

Wrapping a cat in a towel.

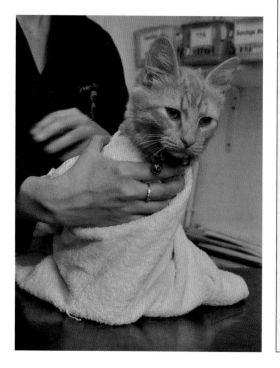

WRAPPING YOUR CAT IN A TOWEL FOR TREATMENT

This is a very useful way of being able to gently restrain your cat whilst you have to give her pills or administer eye or ear drops as it keeps sharp claws tucked away! It is, however, usually a two-person job, so you may have to enlist an assistant. Place your cat in the centre of a large towel on a table. Pull up the front of the towel under her chin and then lift the sides of the towel so that you have fully wrapped your cat (legs, tail and all). You have to be quick, and then lean in over your wrapped-up cat, holding the edges of the towel firmly to prevent her from getting a leg free. Your friend should then be able to apply the eye/ear drops or give the tablet, whilst you have your cat held firmly and safely.

Symptoms of dental disease, such as halitosis and drooling of saliva, can also be signs of other problems such as kidney disease, an oral tumour or even of a foreign body stuck in your cat's mouth.

For these reasons, aside from the fact that dental disease needs early diagnosis and treatment, it is important to have your cat checked by the vet if you have any concerns about the health of her teeth, gums or mouth.

HOW TO ASSESS YOUR CAT'S DENTAL HEALTH

To assess the state of your cat's teeth and gums, gently lift up her lip. Her gums should be a nice healthy pink, her teeth should be fairly white, and her breath not too offensive. Accumulations of brown tartar, a red line at the gum margin and halitosis, bleeding gums or drooling of saliva are all signs that your cat may be suffering from dental disease. If it is severe, your cat may also be finding it painful to eat and may appear to drop her food, not managing dry food at all.

Routine dental care

Plaque will build up on your cat's teeth every day unless you are brushing her teeth to remove it, or she is on a diet whereby it is mechanically removed by chewing. Plaque is invisible to the naked eye and we are only able to see it when it has developed into brown tartar, which cannot be removed by tooth brushing (only by your cat undergoing a 'dental'). In time, tartar causes inflammation of the gums, gingivitis and periodontal disease, which eventually leads to tooth loss.

Tartar build-up caused by plaque can be avoided either by cleaning your cat's teeth yourself using a soft toothbrush or by having your vet scale and polish them under general anaesthesia.

Tooth brushing

There are special toothbrushes designed for use on cats that are especially soft, and you can get ones that fit onto the end of your finger. Using a meat-flavoured pet-friendly toothpaste helps to make the task less unpleasant, and you can begin by rubbing this onto your cat's gums just using your fingers. Pet toothpaste usually contains enzymes that will help to break down plaque and reduce the bacterial load on the gums. Even if your cat will only tolerate the application of the toothpaste, rather than the use of a toothbrush, at least it is moderately beneficial. Unfortunately, unless you get your cat used to having her teeth brushed as a kitten or youngster, it may well be impossible for you to manage it when she is an adult.

Brushing your cat's teeth when she already has gingivitis and periodontal disease will be both ineffective and painful. In such situations she will usually require a dental in order to remove severe accumulations of tartar (as well as any rotten teeth), before you are able to effectively start tooth brushing.

Common dental complaints

Gingivitis

This is the early stage of gum disease where the gums become red and swollen and may bleed. If left untreated, gingivitis can lead to periodontal disease and eventually loss of teeth. Another consequence of gingivitis is that the bacteria from the gums circulate around your cat's entire body and have been linked to systemic conditions such as heart and kidney disease. This means that your cat's overall health can be compromised because of poor dental health, as her immune system will be under constant strain having to battle the infection in her mouth.

To treat gingivitis at an early stage and to help prevent it, routine tooth brushing or the use of raw meaty bones in the diet will be important. At later stages a dental may be required.

Feline odontoclastic resorptive lesions (FORLs)

This is one of the most common dental problems in cats. Lesions develop in the gums causing a lot of pain (and gingivitis), eventually leading to tooth loss. Your vet can identify these lesions in your cat by X-ray and also when she is under general anaesthesia for her dental. Affected teeth will be removed, making your cat much more comfortable than when she had rotten, infected teeth in her mouth. Cats do surprisingly well with teeth missing, and some completely toothless cats can still manage to eat crunchy food!

Stomatitis and ulcers

Stomatitis is an allergic-type reaction thought to be associated with dental plaque, in which the cat's whole mouth becomes sore and swollen. This is a complex disease that usually requires in-depth veterinary treatment.

Complementary treatments for dental disease

Diet: fresh food means healthy digestive processes and sweeter breath. Adding the herbs fennel, peppermint and especially parsley to your cat's diet can help to make her breath smell sweeter.

Homeopathic remedies: Arsenicum album or phosphorus, if the gums bleed easily; mercurius solbuilis, for swollen gums with foul odour. Use at 30c twice daily for five days. Fragaria is also said to help soften tartar, making it easier to remove; use 30c twice daily for three or four weeks.

Supplements: antioxidants, vitamins C and E.

Topical: the following can be rubbed directly onto the gums using your fingers or a cotton bud: manuka honey, propolis or bruised, fresh sage leaves. Alternatively, make up a tincture of Oregon grape, goldenseal, thyme, sage or rosemary. Hypercal solution can be applied to sore gums topically too.

DENTAL TREATMENT

If your cat has severe accumulation of tartar and accompanying periodontal disease she may have to have a 'dental'. This involves a scale and polish, as well as the removal of any rotten teeth by the vet under anaesthetic. After a dental your cat will need to have softer foods for a week or so, whilst her gums are still tender. You can help speed her recovery by giving her arnica 30c twice daily for three to five days after the dental. Also use a hypercal solution rinse if your cat has had extractions, as this has antiseptic and healing properties.

THE DIGESTIVE SYSTEM

Your cat's digestion is finely tuned and can be affected by stress, anxiety, para-

This cat is having intravenous fluids.

lethargic, off her food, has any blood in her stools, or has vomited several times, then she will need to see the vet.

Routine care for digestive complaints

A sudden change in diet can be a common cause of diarrhoea. To help prevent this, make any change to your cat's diet, whether this is just the brand or flavour of food, slowly, over several days. Gradually mix the old food and the new together, until your cat is on 100 per cent new food after around a week. If your cat does get sudden, mild diarrhoea, with no other symptoms, and she is otherwise bright and well in herself, then withhold food for a day and then go back to her original diet. Alternatively, offer her a bland, highly digestible, low-fat diet such as chicken or white fish. You can then gradually reintroduce your cat's usual food after a few days, if all is going well.

Using a probiotic supplement (choose one that is specially formulated for cats, from your vet or the pet shop) can also help to get your cat's digestive system back to normal after a problem such as diarrhoea.

sites, infections, food allergies, physical obstructions and by an imbalance of intestinal microflora. In fact, the role of the digestive system is fundamental to your cat's well-being. If she cannot digest her food properly, then this will result in a cascade of other health problems, as her nutritional needs are not being met, leading to many chronic illnesses having their root cause in digestive disturbances.

Whilst vomiting and diarrhoea can often be mild and self-correcting, they can also be symptoms of a potentially life-threatening problem. Hence, if you are in any doubt, or if your cat shows any symptoms of abdominal pain or discomfort, is

---

ONGOING DIARRHOEA

If your cat's diarrhoea doesn't clear up after a few days, or if it is severe, then she will need to be seen by the vet. Take in a recent stool sample so that your vet can have this analysed at the laboratory for the presence of harmful bacteria, viruses and parasites. This will help to identify the cause of the problem and allow suitable treatment to be instigated.

Common gastrointestinal complaints
Diarrhoea
Diarrhoea can vary in consistency, colour, frequency and in whether it contains any blood or mucus. Diarrhoea caused by problems in the small intestine is usually watery and copious, whereas that caused by problems in the large intestine (colitis) tends to contain mucus. Diarrhoea can have many different causes, ranging from a sudden change in diet, to worms, bacterial infection, poisoning, metabolic disease and even cancer. Hence, diarrhoea is just a symptom of disease, rather than the disease in itself. So your vet will have to find the cause of your cat's diarrhoea by doing a full examination and taking a medical history.

Treatment will, of course, depend on the cause of the diarrhoea and may be as simple as a worming tablet or as complex as an operation or emergency treatment.

Constipation
This can be common, especially in elderly cats. Many factors can contribute to constipation, including diet and inactivity, but also chronic kidney failure and dehydration. The use of a wet food (with the addition of a little extra water) can help to maintain regular bowel function in uncomplicated cases of constipation. Similarly, adding a teaspoon of cooked pumpkin to your cat's food may be helpful in the short term, as it provides extra fibre to help bulk up the stools. Encouraging exercise can help toileting and increase regularity.

If your cat suffers with chronic constipation then the underlying cause needs to be diagnosed by the vet so that it can be treated appropriately. Retained stools in a constipated cat can cause serious consequences, resulting in damage to the nerves and muscles of the colon.

Hair-balls
Hairballs cause your cat to retch and bring up balls of hair that she has ingested through grooming. An occasional hairball is normal, especially in long-haired cats, but if they are a common occurrence (more than once a week), then it needs attention.

Help to prevent hairball problems by grooming your cat regularly using a fine-toothed comb. Common treatment involves use of an indigestible, mineral oil or a proprietary diet that is higher in fibre and formulated to help reduce hairballs. Cats often try to self-medicate to get rid of hairballs by eating grass to make them retch and bring up the hair.

Long-haired cats can be prone to hairballs.

Vomiting
If your cat vomits profusely or persistently, even if she is otherwise well, she should be seen by the vet as this can be a symptom of a number of medical conditions, ranging from the mild to the serious, which will need treatment.

Inflammatory bowel disease
Cats can develop sensitivity to any component of their diet and suffer from

inflammatory bowel disease where they have loose stools, variable appetite and are generally unwell. There can be a wide range of different trigger factors for inflammatory bowel disease, so you will need to discuss the best course of action with your vet. Management of this condition usually involves the use of a special diet to eliminate the causal factors. This may begin with using a novel diet that contains a new source of protein (for example, venison or duck) that your cat has not been fed before, for at least six to eight weeks.

Complementary treatments for digestive complaints
Herbal Remedies: for diarrhoea, slippery elm and plantain can be used to help firm the stools up. They also contain mucilage, which helps to soothe and protect the intestinal lining. Chamomile, peppermint and ginger are other soothing digestive herbs that can help to relieve nausea and vomiting. They can be given as tinctures or infusions.

COMPLEMENTARY TREATMENT FOR TRAVEL SICKNESS

If your cat tends to get nauseous when travelling, then the homeopathic remedy cocculus, 30c, may be useful. One dose can be given two to four hours before the journey, and another just before travel. It can then be repeated every four hours during the journey. You can also give your cat Dr Bach's Rescue Remedy to help relieve anxiety related to travel. Give four drops onto a treat (or directly into your cat's mouth), about forty minutes before the journey.

Homeopathic Remedies: Nux vomica for diarrhoea and vomiting that is due to over-eating or from eating rotten or rancid foods; ipecacuana if there is retching and blood in the vomit; and podophyllum for diarrhoea that is of sudden onset and profuse, watery and exceptionally offensive. These can all be used at 30c potency twice daily for a week.

Supplements: probiotics can help to restore and re-establish the good bacteria in the intestines.

THE RESPIRATORY SYSTEM

The respiratory system includes the nose, windpipe, bronchial tubes and lungs, and it is intimately linked with the cardiovascular system. The body uses sneezing and coughing as a way of expelling debris and infectious agents from the respiratory system. Coughs can differ widely, from the dry to the productive, and from the intermittent tickle to the persistent retching cough.

Due to the wide variety of possible causes, some minor and others very serious, it is important to have any respiratory system problem diagnosed by the vet so that the correct form of treatment can be used.

Common causes of respiratory complaints
Cat flu
Cats can commonly cough and sneeze if they are suffering from 'cat flu', which is caused by the herpes and calici viruses (which are included in their routine vaccinations).

Asthma and other chronic airway complaints
Chronic irritation to the airways is the most common cause of coughing in cats.

145

This is usually diagnosed as feline asthma or allergic bronchitis. However, a persistent or severe cough could also be a sign of a much more serious condition such as pneumonia or heart disease, so careful veterinary diagnosis is always important for any persistently coughing cat.

One of the most successful ways of treating asthmatic cats is to medicate them via the use of a special feline inhaler. These are tolerated surprisingly well by most cats, can be easier to use than having to give tablets, and targets the medications to exactly where they are most needed: the airways.

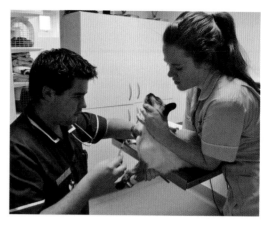

A busy veterinary hospital team at work.

Obstruction/foreign body

Nasal discharge from just one nostril, with accompanying discomfort, may indicate the presence of a foreign body, not uncommonly a blade of grass, lodged up your cat's nose.

Routine care for the respiratory system

You can do a lot to improve the air quality in your home by opening the windows whenever you can and having houseplants to help keep the air clear and pure. Avoid synthetic air fresheners and of course do not smoke near your cat. All these will exacerbate conditions such as asthma. It is also a good idea to change to low-dust type of cat litter.

In some cases of severe cat flu, or if your cat has temporarily lost her sense of smell, she may also be off her food. If this happens, you can help by warming the food to release tempting aromas.

Complementary treatments for respiratory system complaints

Herbal remedies: liquorice acts as an expectorant, so is helpful in productive coughs. Thyme may be suitable for dry coughs and marshmallow (used as a glyc-

etract) has a soothing action on the respiratory tract so may be of benefit for feline asthma.

Homeopathic remedies: Antimonium tartaricum, for rattly coughs with much loose mucus; Arsenicum album for asthmatic coughs and ipecacuana for coughing spasms. For watery nasal discharges and sneezing Allium cepa is indicated. Kali bich is the remedy of choice for nasal discharges that are ropey and yellow, with crusts to the nostrils and violent sneezing. These remedies are used at a 12c or 30c potency twice daily for a week.

Acupuncture: this can be effective at helping to clear the sinuses and boost the immune system.

Supplements: the addition of one teaspoon of manuka honey to your cat's food is both soothing and anti-microbial. For cats with a cough it is also a good idea to soak their dry food, making it less irritating for a sore throat.

THE HEART

Cats can suffer from a number of different heart complaints affecting either the heart muscle itself or the chambers of the heart and the valves and large blood vessels. Unfortunately, due to the sometimes subtle nature of the early signs of disease, these problems can remain undiagnosed until your cat begins to suffer from more dramatic symptoms associated with high blood pressure or blood clots. However, in most cases they would have been suffering for a long time beforehand from more subtle symptoms, including lethargy, breathing difficulties and in some cases coughing (although this is less common than it is in dogs). Your vet may also detect a heart complaint by finding that your cat has an irregular heart rhythm, a weak or irregular pulse, abnormal blood pressure and related symptoms such as fluid in her chest or abdomen.

If you suspect your cat is suffering from any form of heart condition then she needs to be seen by the vet straight away. As with the advice given in the rest of this chapter, the following suggestions for supportive complementary treatments are to be used under veterinary guidance only, and are not intended as sole forms of therapy in serious conditions.

Common heart conditions

Cardiomyopathy

This means disease of the heart muscle and can occur when your cat's heart muscle becomes too thick (as in hypertrophic cardiomyopathy), or if it becomes scarred and fibrotic (as in restrictive cardiomyopathy) – in either case it is less effective at pumping the blood around the body. Hypertrophic cardiomyopathy has been linked to a genetic abnormality in certain breeds of cat, particularly the Ragdoll and the Maine Coon.

Different medications and treatments are given depending on the type of heart disease your cat is suffering from.

HIGH BLOOD PRESSURE

This is relatively common in older cats and can be linked to a number of conditions such as kidney disease and hyperthyroidism. High blood pressure, if left untreated, can have serious effects on your cat's health as it affects the heart and kidneys and can also lead to blindness. It is often possible for your vet to be able to check your cat's blood pressure, and some practices do this as part of their routine health checks for older cats.

Complementary treatments for heart support

Acupuncture: beneficial for heart conditions.

Diet: use potassium-rich foods such as green leafy vegetables (broccoli and spinach). Consider adding fresh (organic) heart to the diet too.

Exercise: keep your cat's weight under control if she suffers from any form of heart condition. Regular, gentle exercise is usually beneficial because it will help to oxygenate the body and stimulate the circulation.

Herbal remedies: hawthorn is the principal heart herb. It helps to improve coronary blood flow, moderate blood pressure and strengthen the heartbeat. Dandelion leaf tea acts as a natural diuretic, helping to rid the body of excess fluid that builds up in cases of congestive heart failure.

Homeopathic remedies: crataegus is a heart support remedy (derived from hawthorn), used daily at a 6c potency or as a tincture.

Supplements: omega-3 fatty acids are very good for the heart; fish oils, such as salmon, are a rich source. Vitamin E and

An integrated veterinary practice.

HYPERTHYROIDISM

This is a very common disease of older cats. It is caused by an increase in the production of thyroid hormones from the thyroid glands in the cat's neck. Thyroid hormones help to control the metabolic rate, so when these are produced in excess your cat's metabolism will speed up. This causes the common symptoms of weight loss despite a ravenous appetite. Your vet will be able to diagnose hyperthyroidism by doing a special blood test. Treatment consists of either surgery, daily medication or in some cases the use of radioactive iodine. If the condition is diagnosed and treated early then most cats respond very well.

selenium are also beneficial. L-carnitine and coenzyme Q10 are other supplements that your vet may recommend.

THE URINARY SYSTEM

The most important job of the urinary system is to get rid of toxic substances and maintain the body's water balance. The kidneys also produce hormones that affect the circulatory system. The bladder is where urine is stored until it is excreted.

Prompt veterinary attention is always warranted with any potential bladder or kidney problem and you should take your cat to the vet if she is showing any signs associated with problems urinating.

General care for the urinary system
In order to maintain a healthy urinary system it is helpful if a significant part of your cat's diet is wet food. This is especially important if your cat has feline lower urinary tract disease (FLUTD), as you will need to encourage her to drink more, as this helps to clear and flush her system. You can do this by adding water to her food and making it a bit mushy, or by soaking her dry food.

You may be able to encourage your cat to drink by getting a water fountain (these are available at pet shops), as some cats prefer to drink from fresh, running water. You should also make sure that she has access to several different water bowls around the house.

Finally, ensure that you give your cat plenty of opportunity to urinate by placing litter trays around the house and making sure that they are emptied regularly. Since overweight and sedentary cats are at increased risk of developing FLUTD, it makes sense to ensure that you encourage your cat to exercise and play and to avoid obesity.

Common complaints of the urinary system

Feline lower urinary tract disease (FLUTD) and feline urological syndrome (FUS)

Feline lower urinary tract disease (FLUTD) or feline urological syndrome (FUS) are the most common diagnoses of urinary problems affecting cats. Either of these terms is used to describe a combination of symptoms associated with irritation to the cat's bladder and urinary tract. These symptoms include painful and frequent urination, changes to your cat's urination habits (such as urinating in odd places around the house), much straining and pain when passing urine, passing blood in the urine and much licking at their genitals.

Despite the fairly common occurrence of these symptoms in cats, the cause of FLUTD is still poorly understood and cannot be identified in every case. Amongst the causes that can be identified are urinary tract infections or tumours (rare), bladder stones or plugs (uncommon), anatomic abnormalities and traumatic damage to the urinary system (also uncommon). In the majority of cases the cause of FLUTD, even after the full range of diagnostic tests have been carried out, is still unknown. These cats are said to be suffering from feline idiopathic or interstitial cystitis (FIC).

If your cat is showing signs of FLUTD your vet will perform diagnostic tests on urine samples and may also take X-rays or perform ultrasound examinations in order to rule out infections and physical blockages to the bladder and urethra (the tube that connects your cat's bladder to the outside), and can then treat her as necessary. Such treatments may include antibiotics, painkillers, a special diet or surgery.

Feline idiopathic cystitis/feline interstitial cystitis (FIC)

This diagnosis is given when no cause for the symptoms of your cat's urinary problems can be identified. Most cases of FIC are recurrent, with your cat likely to suffer from it on and off in the long term.

Treatment of sudden onset episodes of FIC usually involve taking your cat to the vet for painkillers and anti-inflammatories. However, due to the recurrent nature of this problem, long-term management of FIC is crucial in order to help reduce the number and frequency of these acute episodes. This involves a combination of increasing your cat's water intake and reducing stress in her home environment, as anxiety and stress are believed to play a role in the causation and continuation of this disease. (See 'General care for the urinary system' above and 'Environmental modifications' below, for more advice about long-term management.)

Urolithiasis

Uroliths are bladder stones that can cause cystitis and ultimately may even cause a blockage in your cat's bladder or urethra, which can be life-threatening. There are two common types of urolith in cats, 'struvite' (found in alkaline urine) and 'oxalate' (found in acidic urine). If your cat is showing any signs of cystitis (straining to urinate or frequent urination), then your vet will need a urine sample in order to check whether your cat is suffering from uroliths. Diagnosis of this condition may also require X-rays of your cat's bladder.

Treatment to resolve uroliths will depend on the severity of the condition, but usually involves the use of a special prescription diet to change the pH of the urine. In some cases an operation is required to remove large uroliths.

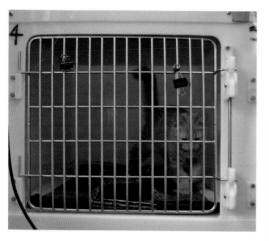

A patient in hospital.

Kidney disease
See Chapter 5.

Complementary treatments for urinary system complaints
Environmental modifications: in addition to the measures outlined above in routine care for the urinary system, as well as helping your cat to increase her daily water consumption, you can also help her to feel relaxed in her home environment by making a few small changes (especially important for cats with FIC). In a multiple-cat household (*see* Chapter 3) it is crucial to ensure that all cats have easy access to their key resources such as food and water bowls, litter trays, high-up resting places, hiding places and escape routes. You may also consider the use of synthetic feline pheromones, such as plug-in diffusers, to help to reduce any feelings of anxiety, which may contribute to conditions such as interstitial cystitis.

Homeopathic remedies: cantharis, if there is extreme straining or blood in the urine; Arsenicum album for cats showing straining and restlessness; Sarsaparilla if the straining is worse at the end of urination. Give at 30c potency twice daily for seven days.

Supplements: glycosaminoglycans are a nutraceutical that can help relieve the symptoms of FLUTD in cats, and may be beneficial as part of long-term manage-

EMERGENCY!

Complete blockage of the urethra can be potentially lethal if not treated quickly. Symptoms that your cat is 'blocked' include trying to pass urine but with no urine or just a few drops being passed, severe pain, lethargy and collapse. Male cats tend to be more at risk of blockage than female cats as they have a much narrower urethra. If you are at all concerned that your cat may be blocked this is an emergency and you must get immediate veterinary assistance.

Signs of pain can include a tendency to sleep more often.

ment as they help to maintain a healthy bladder wall.

Cranberry juice is often used for dogs with cystitis because it helps prevent bacteria from adhering to the bladder wall. However, in cats cystitis is rarely linked to a bacterial infection, so this is less beneficial.

THE MUSCULOSKELETAL SYSTEM

The musculoskeletal system comprises the muscles, ligaments, bones and joints. The most common problem affecting your cat's mobility is arthritis. This is inflammation of a joint, causing pain and stiffness. The most common form of arthritis is osteoarthritis, also called degenerative joint disease. This is usually an age-related degeneration of joint cartilage affecting elderly cats, causing pain, stiffness and reduced mobility (*see* Chapter 5).

Most joint pain occurs due to either loss of or damage to cartilage or joint fluid, or to the deposition of extra bone within the joint. Any of these situations leads to bone rubbing against bone, as well as a swollen joint capsule, both of which are painful. Signs that your cat may be suffer-

ing from joint pain and arthritis include a tendency to sleep more and move around less, to avoid or hesitate when jumping up onto favourite places such as chairs or windowsills, and not wanting to be stroked or groomed over certain painful areas of the body. Some of the signs that your cat is suffering may be subtle, as they are very good at hiding symptoms of discomfort.

Cats can also suffer from dislocations and fractures (often after road traffic accidents, for instance), as well as from problems affecting her muscles, ligaments or tendons, all of which can result in pain and lameness.

A cat suffering from sudden onset (or ongoing) pain and stiffness should be taken to a vet – she may require X-rays or other diagnostic tests.

Routine care for musculoskeletal complaints

If your cat is suffering from pain or stiffness, it is helpful to make adjustments to her home environment so that getting around is easier for her and she can still readily access her favourite resting places, beds, litter trays and feeding stations. Keeping your cat's weight down is important if she suffers from arthritis, as obesity will put extra strain on her joints.

Common musculoskeletal problems
Arthritis
See Chapter 5.

Fractures
If your cat has sustained a fracture, this will usually be diagnosed through X-ray and treated either with orthopaedic surgery or by rest and conservative management, depending on the site and severity of the injury. Your cat may also be required to spend a period of time confined to a small space, such as a crate or a small pen, to help with rest and recuperation.

Sprains and strains
Your cat can strain or sprain various ligaments due to accidents or injuries sustained whilst climbing trees or jumping over garden fences, for example. Your vet will help to diagnose these injuries. The most common treatment involves rest and the use of anti-inflammatories and painkillers. Certain homeopathic remedies (*see* 'complementary treatment', below) may also be indicated.

Injury and infection
Sudden severe lameness can also result from injury to your cat's footpads, for example from thorns or from walking on hot tarmac in the summer. It can also arise from cat bite injury (through fighting) to the lower limb. This can cause cellulitis and associated abscesses, which are very painful and can cause lameness.

Complementary treatment for musculoskeletal complaints
Chiropractic treatment: this is beneficial in many cases as it addresses the knock-on effects of altered mobility, for example where long-term lameness in one limb has caused extra weight or strain on another limb (or along the spine), and hence results in more complex problems than just the original injury.

Physiotherapy: often used as part of a rehabilitation programme to help build up function and regain range of movement.

Acupuncture: a natural form of pain relief that addresses underlying predisposing factors.

Herbal remedies: turmeric and devil's claw are two of the most recognized anti-

MAKING THE CAT CARRIER A FRIEND

Cats do not like leaving their familiar territory, and this makes a trip to the vet even more terrifying for them, as it is a voyage into the unknown. It is also true that because of their highly tuned sense of balance, cats find a trip in the car more unpleasant than it would be for other animals such as dogs. The car will also sound and smell very different, again making them feel uneasy and scared. Cats that were taken in the car as kittens, between the ages of three and seven weeks, when they are most receptive to learning new things, are usually much better travellers as adults. Make the cat carrier more inviting by leaving it out in the house for your cat to go into, and out of, of her own accord – rather than keeping it in the loft and only getting it down when you are taking your cat to the vet! Make it enticing for your cat to go into by placing treats in it.

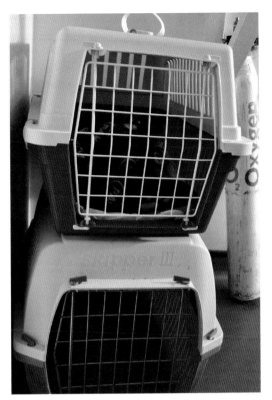

The cat carrier.

inflammatory herbs. Comfrey is considered a classic bone and joint repair herb.

Homeopathic remedies: rhus tox, ruta and arnica can be used as a combined remedy (often called 'RRA'), for treatment of pain and stiffness that eases up on initial movement, or for sprains and strains. Ruta grav is the indicated remedy for ligament or tendon strain, Bellis perennis for deep muscle injury, and hamamelis for bruises, strains and sprains. These can be given at 30c twice daily for several weeks. Don't forget arnica used in a high potency (200c) straight after any injury (to help with shock as well as bruising). After one or two doses change to 30c twice daily.

Supplements: antioxidants (vitamins C and E), and glucosamines and chondroitin are indicated for long-term support. (*See* Chapter 8.)

FIRST AID

The secret of first aid is to 'be prepared'. Having a first aid kit for your cat, and knowing how to use what you have in it, is crucial. It is worth while finding a course in animal first aid (ask your vet) where you can learn the basics of first aid and how to care for your pets.

Whilst minor wounds can be treated at home, if they worsen, or your cat is in pain or has any other symptoms, then the vet must see her straight away. It is best to ring your vet first. Have a pen to hand as you may need to write down a different telephone number, especially if you are contacting them out of hours, as you may be given instructions to take your cat to a different surgery.

Complementary treatments for first aid
Abscesses
To encourage an abscess to burst, use the homeopathic remedy hepar sulph twice daily at 12c. After they have burst, bathe abscesses with hypercal solution.

Bites and stings
Apis mel and ledum are two homeopathic remedies used for wasp and bee stings to help relieve the stinging and swelling. Give 30c every ten to fifteen minutes until resolved (or for a maximum of five doses).

Bruising
Arnica is the number one homeopathic remedy for bruising. Use 200c for one or two doses in acute situations, and then 30c for twice daily dosing. Arnica cream can be used on bruises too, but never

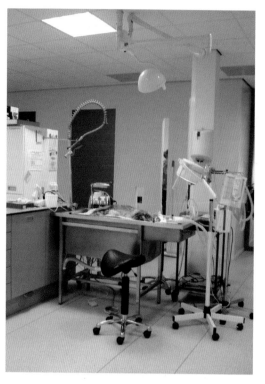

The veterinary hospital.

Cuts/lacerations

Bath or flush with hypercal solution and then bandage as necessary. Use hypercal cream topically twice or three times daily.

Ripped claws/nails

Clean and bathe them with a solution of hypercal and give the remedy hypericum by mouth (200c or 30c) as well, to help with nerve pain.

apply it to open wounds.

Burns

Hold the area under cool running water. Give the homeopathic remedy cantharis 30c every ten to fifteen minutes until resolved (or for a maximum of five doses). Use urtica urens cream for topical use.

Crushed digits/tail

For injuries involving sensitive nerve endings, such as crush-type injuries (your cat's feet getting stepped on or having something dropped on them, or having their tail trapped in a door), use the homeopathic remedy hypericum (30 or 200c).

CASE STUDY: ROAD TRAFFIC ACCIDENT

Lucky, a four-year-old black cat, was found by his owners at the side of the road, having just been hit by a car. They immediately scooped him up very gently, using a thick towel, and rang their vet to say that they were on their way. As they got into the car with Lucky, they gave him four drops of Dr Bach's Rescue Remedy, using the pipette to place the drops inside the corner of his mouth. They also gave one drop of the homeopathic remedy aconite (200c). These complementary remedies helped Lucky counter the shock of the accident and were given on the way to the vet.

Shock

Use Dr Bach's Rescue Remedy, four drops every ten to fifteen minutes, or the homeopathic remedy aconite (at a high potency, 200c), giving two or three doses.

Strains and sprains

Use the homeopathic remedy ruta grav (30c) for tendon or ligament injury.

Wounds

Use hypercal solution to bathe wounds. This is a homeopathic antiseptic solution that you can either buy ready made up, or you can make yourself by taking the tinctures of calendula and hypericum and diluting them one or two drops in approximately 500ml sterile saline. Calendula cream is excellent for helping wounds to heal and should be applied to the area three times a day. Manuka honey can be applied to wounds as a natural antibiotic and antiseptic. Aloe vera is another option; it has a soothing and healing action.

YOUR FIRST AID KIT
Aconite liquid remedy (200c)
Aloe vera gel
Arnica tablets (30c and 200c)
Bandages
Calendula cream
Hypercal tincture
Manuka honey
Rescue Remedy
Urtica cream
Witch Hazel
Sterile saline solution
Blunt tipped scissors
Tweezers
Tick remover
Gauze pads
Roll of adhesive bandage (or vet wrap)
Thick towel (you can use this to wrap your cat in to ease handling)
Emergency vet's telephone number taped inside the kit
Always make sure your cat carrier is easily accessible, in case you need to use it in an emergency.

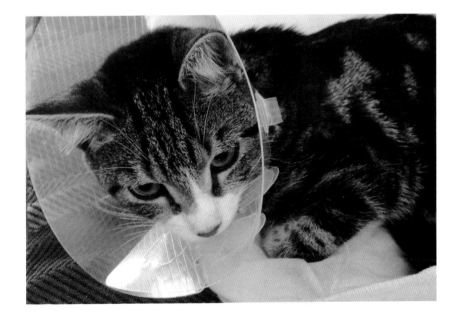

Wearing a buster collar prevents this cat from licking her wounds.

USEFUL ADDRESSES

Acupuncture
The Association of British Veterinary Acupuncturists, BMAS House,
3 Winnington Court, Northwich,
CW8 1AQ
Telephone: 01606 786782
Website: www.abva.co.uk

Bach Flower Remedies
The Bach Centre, Mount Vernon,
Bakers Lane, Brightwell-cum-Sotwell,
Oxon, OX10 OPZ
Telephone: 01491 834678
Website: www.bachcentre.com

Herbalism
The British Association of Veterinary Herbalists.
Website: www.herbalvets.org.uk

The National Institute of Medical Herbalists (NIMH), Elm House,
54 Mary Arches Street, Exeter,
EX4 3BA
Telephone: 01392 426 022
Website: www.nimh.org.uk

Homoeopathy
The British Association of Homoeopathic Veterinary Surgeons (BAHVS).
Website: www.bahvs.com

The British Homoeopathic Association, Hahnemann House, 29 Park Street West,
Luton, LU1 3BE
Telephone: 01582 408675
Website: www.britishhomoeopathy.org

Suppliers of Homoeopathic Remedies
Ainsworth's Homoeopathic Pharmacy, 36 New Cavendish Street, London, W1G 8UF
Telephone: 0207 467 5435
Website: www.ainsworths.com

Freeman's Homoeopathic Pharmacy, 18–20 Main Street, Busby, Glasgow, G76 8DU
Telephone: 0845 22 55 1 55
Website: www.freemans.co.uk

McTimoney Chiropractic
The McTimoney Chiropractic Association,
Crowmarsh Gifford, Wallingford,
Oxfordshire, OX10 8DJ
Telephone: 01491 829211
Website: www.mctimoneychiropractic. org

Rescue Cats
Cats Protection, National Cat Centre,
Chelwood Gate, Haywards Heath,
Sussex, RH17 7TT
Telephone: 03000 121212
Website: www.cats.org.uk

Tellington Touch
Tilley Farm, Timsbury Road,
Farmborough, Somerset, BA2 0AB
Telephone: 01761 471182
Website: www.tilleyfarm.co.uk

Veterinary Surgeons
The Royal College of Veterinary Surgeons, Belgravia House, 62–64 Horseferry Road, London, SW19 2AF
Telephone: 0207 222 2001
Website: www.rcvs.org.uk

FURTHER READING

Fogle, B. *Natural Cat Care* (Dorling Kindersley, 1999)

Fougere, B. *The pet lover's guide to natural healing for cats and dogs* (Elsevier Saunders, 2006)

Hamilton, D. *Homeopathic care for cats and dogs – small doses for small animals* (North Atlantic Books, 1999)

Riccomini, F. *Know your cat* (Hamlyn, 2008)

Schwartz, C. *Four paws, five directions – a guide to Chinese medicine for cats and dogs* (Celestial Arts Publishing, 1996)

Tilford, G. and Wulff, M. *Herbs for pets – the natural way to enhance your pet's life* (Bowtie Press, 2009)

ACKNOWLEDGEMENTS

There isn't room enough to mention everyone who has helped and supported me, but I would like to say a special thank-you to the following people: Holly Smith, Sarah Compson, Jane Compson, Hester Page, Bill Moore, Alicia Decina, Natasha Milne, Jillian Laird and Sandy Peacock, Nuala Smith, Helena Wooltorton, Laurie Gethin, Deep Sehgal, Naomi Woodspring and Nick Shipton, Sara Blackmore and Fanny Peppercorn.

Also a huge thank-you to Green Pastures Veterinary Centre, Highcroft Vets and to Mrs Alison Webster for kindly giving us permission to reproduce 'On a Cat, Ageing'.

INDEX